P9-DNO-334

GROUNDWORK GUIDES

Slavery Today
Kevin Bales &
Becky Cornell
The Betrayal of
Africa
Gerald Caplan
Sex for Guys
Manne Forssberg
Technology
Wayne Grady
Hip Hop World
Dalton Higgins
Democracy
James Laxer
Empire
James Laxer
Oil
James Laxer
Cities
John Lorinc
Pornography
Debbie Nathan
Being Muslim
Haroon Siddiqui

Genocide
Jane Springer
The News
Peter Steven
Gangs
Richard Swift
Climate Change
Shelley Tanaka
The Force of Law
Mariana Valverde

Series Editor
Jane Springer

GROUNDWORK GUIDES

Gangs
Richard Swift

Groundwood Books
House of Anansi Press

Toronto Berkeley

Groundwood Books / House of Anansi Press
110 Spadina Avenue, Suite 801, Toronto, Ontario M5V 2K4
or c/o Publishers Group West
1700 Fourth Street, Berkeley, CA 94710

We acknowledge for their financial support of our publishing
program the Canada Council for the Arts, the Government of Canada through
the Canada Book Fund (CBF) and the Ontario Arts Council.

This book was written with the support of an Ontario Arts Council Writers'
Reserve Grant.

 Canada Council   Conseil des Arts
for the Arts   du Canada

 ONTARIO ARTS COUNCIL
CONSEIL DES ARTS DE L'ONTARIO

Library and Archives Canada Cataloguing in Publication
Swift, Richard
Gangs / Richard Swift.
(Groundwork guides)
ISBN 978-0-88899-979-5 (bound).--ISBN 978-0-88899-978-8 (pbk.)
1. Gangs. 2. Crime prevention. I. Title. II. Series: Groundwork guides
HV6437.S84 2011   364.106'6   C2010-905904-2

Design by Michael Solomon
Typesetting by Sari Naworynski
Index by Gillian Watts

Contents

1 Gangs Are Everywhere 7

2 Gangs and Poverty 26

3 The Underground Economy 41

4 Gangs and Their Communities 56

5 Gang Appeal 68

6 The Politics of Gangs 80

7 The Assault on Youth 93

8 A Future with Gangs 108

Gang Vocabulary 126

Gangs Timeline 127

Notes 129

For Further Information 136

Acknowledgments 138

Index 139

To Joshua — far too skeptical to ever join a gang.

Chapter 1
Gangs Are Everywhere

> Almost everyone has their weapons, and when you
> go out into the street you never know if you're
> going to return, what's going to happen to you,
> when they're going to assault you. You don't have
> security — we don't live in peace… There have
> only been deaths.
>
> — Maria, aged 20, Guatemala City[1]

Politicians. Police. Teachers. The media. Social workers. The elderly. Solid citizens everywhere. Everyone
these days is alarmed about youth gangs. Next to terrorists, gangs are the number two "other" — a mani-
festation of pure evil. The media is filled with stories
about youth in gangs — drug-dealing, terrorizing
neighborhoods, gunning down each other as well as a
growing number of bystanders. In the Paris *banlieues*
(suburbs) they set cars alight, in downtown Toronto
they open up with handguns on the subway cars or
in crowded downtown streets, in Birmingham and
Warsaw they rampage after football matches, and in

many parts of the world they turn entire urban areas into no-go zones for the police.

Throughout burgeoning slums of the urban Global South, in cities as far apart as Rio de Janeiro in Brazil and Nairobi in Kenya, gangs of young men and sometimes women are the most important form of social organization in young people's lives. They have come to replace the religious institutions that play such a large role in the lives of their parents and grandparents. And as the Global South rapidly shifts its population from the slow, predictable rhythms of rural life to the volatile speed-up of urban life, gangs and their impact are only likely to grow.

For the young, in particular, gangs provide moorings in a world set adrift. The city appears dangerous and exciting but also a rupture from the old certainties of parents and grandparents. Traditional families under pressure of a new kind of confusing urban poverty often end up neglecting or abusing children, driving them out into the street in search of opportunity and companionship. The old ways and customs of respect and belief no longer seem to apply, and youth gangs provide both a social rooting and a sense of identity for young people torn between their dreams and the stark realities of the poverty that hems them in. The economic possibilities provided by gang life (mostly but not all criminal) are a crucial factor in what draws the young into gangs. And economics is behind the persistence of those gangs as a part of the social landscape in the slums of both the Global South and the Global North.

What's in a Name?

What outsiders call these gangs or what the gangs call themselves varies from place to place. In Latin America they are known as *pandillas, maras, bandas, galeras, quadrillas, baras* and *chapulines*. In Jamaica they are known as "posses," dating back to the 1970s when *Bonanza* TV show reruns hit Caribbean television.

What the gangs call themselves reveals how they view the world and their place in it. Gang names dot newspaper columns as well as police blotters and court charge sheets. In countries like East Timor, plagued by youth gang violence since the country's independence from Indonesia, they go by names like Devoted Heart Lotus Brotherhood and Sagrada Família (holy family). In São Luís, capital of the northeastern Brazilian state of Maranhão, youth gangs call themselves Messengers from Hell, Mind Organizers, Terrible Nocturnals and Falta de Deus (absence of God).

Gang names serve a number of purposes — to strike fear in the hearts of outsiders or competitors, but also to establish an outcast identity and to promote internal loyalty. For example, Amigos dos Amigos (ADA, meaning friends of friends), which controls Roçinha, the largest favela (slum) in Rio de Janeiro, speaks to group solidarity.[2]

Many gangs have names with religious echoes. They sometimes evoke a rejection of God but more often use terms like "disciples," which suggest a longing for certainties in an uncertain world. Others like Falta de Deus speak of a lack of religion or even abandonment by God.

The massive gang-ridden Cape Flats slum near the South African city of Cape Town is home to an estimated 130 different gangs, including the Hard Livings, the Mongrels and the Junky Funky Boys.

The biggest of the Cape Flats gangs is called the Americans, evoking not just the power of US gangs, but the cultural domination of the powerful US film and music industries. A gang in the US city of Cincinnati called the Northside Taliban has its own rap song on YouTube. There is even a website, www.gangnames.net, featuring names for US-based gangs — you can vote on the best ones or submit your own.[3] In Germany and Russia gangs tend to cluster around anti-foreigner activity. One Russian gang calling itself the White Inquisitor's Crew has a record of attacking Chinese, Uzbek and other groupings from the east of the country. Skinhead gangs tend toward names that promote a Nazi revival, while some German gangs like the Pomeranian Homeland Association maintain innocuous names to hide their neo-Nazi inclinations.

Youth Gang Explosion

There are many types of gangs, ranging from sophisticated international criminal cartels to the famous motorcycle gangs like the Hell's Angels or the Satan's Choice that prowl on North American highways. But this book concentrates on the youth gangs that number in the tens of thousands and are present in a growing number of cities around the world.

Gang organization is limited by the political space available. For example, highly administered societies like Iran and China and Singapore allow little room for gang activity, but the collapse of orthodox Communism has provided fruitful opportunities in Russia and other states of the former Soviet Union. There tend to be fewer gangs in societies with a strong religious orientation, particularly Islamic (including most of the Middle East) but also Christian ones (Ghana, for example). There is also less space for self-organized youth gangs where the criminal scene is dominated by adult gangs such as the narco-traffickers in Colombia and Mexico. Countries with extensive social welfare networks, such as those of Northern Europe, are also less likely to have an extensive gang presence. But youth gangs are on the rise elsewhere in Europe.

European gangs, referred to in France as *bandes*, are often drawn from either guest worker populations (Turkish gangs in Germany) or former colonies (Latin American gangs such as the Latin Kings in Madrid and Barcelona) or both, as with sub-Saharan African gangs in Belgium or North African and sub-Saharan gangs in France or "yardie" Caribbean gangs and South Asian gangs in the UK.

The typical youth gang, although varied in size and impact, is generally territorially based in a particular community, neighborhood or urban district. The grandfather of gang studies, Frederic Thrasher, after studying more than a thousand gangs in 1920s Chicago, warned that "no two gangs are just alike, [there is] an endless variety of forms."[4]

It is useful to see gangs on a continuum, moving from sporadic and informal gangs to institutionalized gangs that are deeply imbedded for decades in the particular communities of (mostly) major cities. The one pole tends to have a lot of ebb and flow, with gang organization quite informal and with limited economic ambitions; at the other end there is more structured leadership (complete with ranks) and an organization that relies on a variety of illegal (and sometimes legal) income streams to sustain itself.

But all along this spectrum there has been a dramatic explosion of both the number of gangs and the number of young people connected to them. Police statistics for the United States alone in 2004 claim 760,000 gang members and 24,000 gangs in 29,000 jurisdictions (legal talk for towns and cities). This marks a 660 percent growth in US gang membership over 24 years.[5]

In 2006 there were 103 illegal organizations (mostly violent youth gangs) in Rivers State in Nigeria's oil-rich Delta region. In El Salvador there were 17,000 arrests (but only 5 percent convictions) of suspected gang members in 2005. According to Mauricio Gaborit of the Central American University in El Salvador, Honduras has taken a regional lead in gang membership. For Gaborit the eruption of violence in Honduras is due to a society fractured into two disparate social categories: one with money and another without the basics of life. His studies indicate that there are over 70,000 youthful members of the Maras in Central America: 40,000 in Honduras, 14,000 in Guatemala, 10,000 in El Salvador and the remaining 6,000 scattered in Nicaragua and Costa Rica.[6]

South Africa, East Timor, the Philippines, Kenya, Haiti, Jamaica, Trinidad, Nigeria and Papua New Guinea all have serious youth gang problems. In the industrial world New Zealand, the UK, Canada and the countries of the former Soviet sphere have seen the most dramatic growth. It is notoriously difficult to get accurate figures on gang membership. The rise and fall of crime rates and arrests (often unfairly placed at the door of young criminals) is not an accurate indicator. But if the evidence of police and other official concern, popular culture and the media are taken as proof, there is a massive global rise in youth gang activity.

History of Youth Gangs

Of course youth gangs aren't new phenomena. In medieval Western Europe gangs of unruly young men were associated with religious abbeys who recruited them. Known as the Abbeys of Misrule, they battled against each other for the honor of their particular abbey and intimidated troublesome villagers.

The derivation of the word "thug," often used to describe young gangsters, comes from the Indian phenomena of "thuggees," referring to youth gangs in thirteenth-century India who used to strangle and rob strangers.

In fourteenth- and fifteenth-century England, gangs like the Mims, Hectors, Bugles and Dead Boys ran amuck in towns and cities, breaking up taverns and battling among themselves. They may have been the first gangs with their own colors in the form of vibrant ribbons to denote gang affiliation.

In the United States the modern forms of youthful street gangs were often associated with particular immigrant communities. The Irish gangs of New York, such as the Dead Rabbits and the Pug Uglies, fought for turf and status (and to gain political power) in the mid-nineteenth century. They were joined by Jewish, Italian and black gangs who organized at least initially for self-protection during the period of the US Civil War. US street gangs were very much tied up with struggles by different ethnic groups to control municipal politics.

There are antecedents to contemporary youth gangs in virtually every national history. In the townships of apartheid South Africa (particularly around Johannesburg) young black men formed themselves into gangs called *tsotsi* in the early part of the twentieth century. Some, known as "protectors," restricted their criminal activity to the white population. Such gangs dominated the world of township youth from the 1930s until the early 1970s.

In the 1950s Maori gangs active in New Zealand were seen as a major source of juvenile crime. In the 1960s two youth gangs in the UK — the Mods (a "posh" fashion-conscious crew) and the Rockers (more influenced by the styles of rock and US motorcycle gangs) — scandalized official society and clashed with each other, particularly at seaside resorts like Clacton-on-Sea.

Most gangs from earlier periods tend to be episodic and lack the kind of rooted presence of contemporary super-gangs.

Blowback

Chicago and Los Angeles eventually emerged as the classic gang cities of North America. Both cities' early dominant youth gangs were made up of black and Latino youth — more Puerto Rican in the case of Chicago gangs like the Latin Kings or the Vice Lords, and more Mexican in LA, where early Hispanic gangs emerged.

Both LA and Chicago were marked by a high degree of racial separation and "neighborhoods of exclusion," to use Loïc Wacquant's phrase in *Urban Outcasts*, a study of the *fin-de-siècle* hyperghetto on Chicago's South and West sides. Wacquant describes a combination of circumstances — the decline in full-time unionized employment, the retreat from welfare commitments to help the poor, and conscious policies of racial and class segregation — that have created a particular type of hopeless poverty in many US cities. He makes the case that a similar process is going on in European countries like France.[7]

The idea of the abandoned urban outcast — of rootless youth facing exclusion and discrimination — spreads far beyond the areas covered in Wacquant's study. The demographic shift that reached its tipping point in 2008 now has the majority of people living in cities for the first time in human history. Most of these people live in precarious economic circumstances without regular employment. Many have no security in their living situations. As squatters they have slapped up makeshift dwellings with few municipal services and are often under constant threat of being expropriated by government or developers. Urban squatter settlements throughout the Global South are the places that the surplus population (no job + no money to consume = no value to society) are dumped. Many squatters and their movements struggle hard to improve their communities and get access to resources. But such communities are also fertile ground for the development of youth gangs.

The street gang is not just a creation of the shanty-towns of the Global South. It is arguably Los Angeles — identified with Hollywood and the export of the American Dream to the furthest reaches of the globe — that is the other key exporter of "gangsta" culture. This is not just through the violent gaming and rap music industries, but through gangsters themselves. Today LA is identified with the Crips and the Bloods and increasingly, ethnic Salvadoran, Honduran and Guatemalan gangs such as the notorious Mara Salvatrucha (MS-13) and Calle 18, or 18th Street Gang (M-18).

The Maras take their name from the marabunta ants, Central American army ants that devour everything in their path. *Trucha* (trout) is Spanish slang for a shrewd person. The Maras are considered super-gangs because of their presence both in North and Central America. They started up in Los Angeles but spread outside the US when the short-sighted zero-tolerance policy in California led to gang members being deported to countries like El Salvador and Honduras, even though they had spent most of their lives and had certainly learned the gang trade there. Central American authorities weren't even told of the criminal records of the thousands of deportees landing on their doorsteps.

The Maras thrived in poverty-ridden conditions with governments and police forces unprepared and under-equipped to deal with them. They established themselves with the use of force in the drug trade and the human-trafficking business — where they prey on desperately poor workers risking their meager savings (and often their lives) to try and get into the US. Many hard-core Maras developed the ability to get back across the border and created a presence throughout many parts of urban and suburban US and Canada — particularly places with a significant Salvadoran population.

This is an example of "blowback," a term used to explain how supposedly high-minded US actions outside its borders result in negative consequences within the US itself. The notion of blowback gained currency when the US was exposed to the antipathy and terror of Al Qaeda and other fundamentalists because of that country's uncritical support of Israel and brutal dictatorships in the Muslim world. In the case of the Maras, militant US anti-immigration attitudes (deport the troublemakers!)

have gone some way to producing a cross-border gang threat.

The Maras are unusual in the recent history of youth gangs, because most remain rooted in the places that they originated. There is a myth that a few big gangs colonize other areas to expand drug and other criminal markets. This is partly because local gangs use the names and symbols of better-known gangs (e.g., Crips, Bloods, Maras, Latin Kings) in order to inflate their reputations. But someone who calls themselves a Crip or a Blood in Toronto or a Mara in St. Louis or Amsterdam likely has nothing to do with the home base of such gangs in Los Angeles or El Salvador.

Most gang analysts believe that gangs are by and large homegrown. If they do move the reason is often to be close to family and friends. Thus blowback, where it occurs, can be seen most frequently as a product of the clampdown by authorities that forces movement to another country or another part of the same country.

What Is a Gang?
Youth gangs vary greatly in their size, methods of operation and values. Each case needs to be looked at in the community and national context from which it arose to understand both its potential and the most effective policies for dealing with gang violence. The best definition of gangs is a general one. Here is how US sociologist John M. Hagedorn describes them in *A World of Gangs*:

Simply alienated groups socialized by the streets and prisons…young people, particularly armed young men, are everywhere filling the void left by weak, repressive, racist or illegitimate states.[8]

All definitions blur at the edges. At the one end we have all probably been part of a gang, or at least a clique, especially as adolescents. Many of us have also done things that were illegal in that context — skipped school, engaged in underage drinking, smoked marijuana, trespassed, got into fights. For some it gets more serious and the transition to a proper street gang begins to occur. This is to some degree conditioned by individual inclination and a search for personal identity but even more so by family circumstances, shaped by conditions of poverty, racism and a lack of opportunity. From there the situation becomes a process, moving from fairly informal street gangs engaged in illegal and sometimes violent defense of a local turf to institutionalized and powerful gangs that control entire sectors of a city and wield considerable economic and even political power. Police and other coercive interventions have been markedly unsuccessful in stopping this trend.

In the Global North (outside the United States) the institutionalized gang is a rarity. Even in cities with a "gang problem," such as Toronto or suburban Paris, gangs come and go, lack stable ranks and structures, and are not embedded in the economy of the communities in which they operate. Most adolescents have only a passing familiarity with these gangs and are not tempted to become members. Those who do become members (if they are not killed or jailed) pass through the gang experience and leave it behind after their mid to late twenties. This does not mean such gangs are harmless — they may at times be more violent than institutionalized gangs that try and control their members and focus on the main task of making a profit for the gang leadership.

The non-institutionalized gang is a good example of what we might call "disorganized crime." Institutionalized street gangs tend to take root in situations where the state and its police and other services are largely absent from the community for extended periods of time. Neglect allows such gangs to flourish, although they never attain the sophistication and violent reach of adult gangs like the Mafia or the narco-traffickers of Colombia and Mexico.

Gang Romance

It is easy to imagine, given their overwhelming bad press, that almost everyone has negative feelings about gangs. This is simply not true. The storied gangs of the Wild West — the James Brothers and Billy the Kid — have long been part of North American popular culture. History is dotted with Robin Hood-type legends of what British historian Eric Hobsbawm calls "social bandits," who by reputation (if not always in fact) fought the oppressors — be they bad kings, ruthless landlords, foreign invaders — and took the side of the people.[9] Most such bandits were young men similar to the fourteen- to twenty-five-year olds who make up modern-day youth gangs.

Hobsbawm's extensive historical investigation of social bandits shows them arising out of marginalized rural communities or as outlawed victims of the political and economic forces that dominated society. His sympathy toward them and the narrow options they faced in life and their choice of rebellion is tempered by a healthy realism about the limitations of their revolt.

The outlaw has always had a romantic following, particularly in those who see the law as something that excludes them from the wealth and power it mostly defends. The success of revolutionaries like Mexican Pancho Villa or Spanish anarchist Sabate, highwaymen like Ned Kelly of Australia or Dick Turpin of England, or the bands that preyed on the wealthy from the mountains of Sardinia to those of Colombia and Peru was in large part due to a popular local following that often protected them from the authorities.

This seems a long way from the brutality of the street gangs that dominate Rio's favelas or vigilante gangs, such as the Bakassi Boys, who terrorize the Niger Delta in Nigeria. But is it? Street gangs of youth are not without their supporters, at least to some degree, because they are seen by many as a force for order in situations where the legitimate government has either withdrawn or is so corrupt and brutal that gangs are a "lesser evil." It is not just fear that keeps gangs like the Crips and the Bloods of Los Angeles a force to be reckoned with but the widespread belief throughout the city's black communities that the Los Angeles Police Department acts as a racist occupying force.

Incidents such as the brutal beating by police officers of the black motorist Rodney King (caught on video camera) and the subsequent beating of black protest demonstrators makes the formula of good police versus bad gangs a bit too easy. This is not to lionize these often brutal gangs. Indeed, contemporaries of Hobsbawm's social bandits of decades or centuries past commonly portrayed them as ruthless thugs and murderers in a manner not dissimilar to the media portrayal of today's youth gangs. But it is essential to understand that today's youth gangs arise out of a social context of poverty, violence and neglect.

Reality Trumps Romance

The penny press that made heroes of Dick Turpin and Jesse James has its modern-day equivalent in the music companies that peddle nihilistic "gangsta rap" around the world as a kind of glorification of the gang lifestyle:

> *Broken dreams and broken homes, we always had issues*
> *And mad problems worshippin gangstas and*
>   *bankrobbers...*
> *Its funny how the money make the whole world love you*
> *Jealous cats hate you, dime pigeons*
> *Little ghetto children run up on you, wanna touch you.*[10]

In the anomie of urban poverty and cultural drift, where gangs provide a sense of identity, it is not surprising that young people are attracted by such messages. There is also a gender element to gang membership. Many young males join gangs because they believe it is a way to attract women.

The "bad boy" image is associated with a degree of sex appeal and the powerful male image linked to guns and violence holds cachet in some circles. This warrior image is also part of mainstream culture. For example, in 1990-91, during the First Gulf War, the balding and pudgy commander of US troops General Schwarzkopf was picked by a survey of women in the US as "the sexiest man in America." As one Toronto-based gang worker points out, "Those who work with gangs will tell you that a large percentage of inter- and intra-gang violence is over girls."[11]

Still, gang life is a long way from its romantic portrayals in music and film. It is often, as they say, nasty, brutish and short. While there may be those who do well out of gang life, for the majority it is a pretty hard slog. Selling "rock and blow" on a cold Chicago street corner for the Latin Kings is likely to earn you about as much as you would make working the same hours at McDonald's.

Most of the people who die in gang violence are members of the gangs themselves. Gang members kill or maim members of different gangs in turf fights or simply because of respect issues. Once you join a gang it is difficult to quit since in many gangs quitting is not an acceptable option. In Brazil, Nigeria, Colombia or South Africa gang members may become targets for vigilantes whose main purpose is to eliminate criminals without having to resort to the legal niceties of arrest and trial. In short, it's a risky life.

Occasionally a more realistic portrayal of gang life rises to the surface, such as the award-winning HBO series *The Wire,* about youth gang life in Baltimore, or the anti-gang videos on YouTube, such as the graphic *Bloods and Crips Shooting* video. In this video Crips line up on one side of a grave, Bloods on the other. Whenever one gets to the front of the line he is shot and falls into the grave. After about two minutes and many bodies one of the young gangsters yells, "Stop! Why are we doing this?"

It doesn't take kids long to figure out the negatives of gang life. The website www.gangstyle.com is full of heartrending testimony from gang members filled with regret and pain. But still the attraction of easy money and a decent amount of respect where both things are in chronically short supply can override the harsh realities.

A great deal of mainstream sociology and criminology attempts to bring together the main causes for gang organization and activity. By and large such approaches look at gang membership as an individual pathology. The solution is to identify potential young offenders at an early age and "treat" them through a series of measures: counseling, pharmaceuticals, incarceration and probation.

A burgeoning industry aims at early identification of "high-risk" youth and exercising control over them.

This may take quite benign forms — for example, the Montreal Preventive Treatment Program begins to tackle disruptive violent behavior in kindergarten, with some success. But the zero-tolerance approach — school expulsions, lengthy prison sentences, heavy-handed policing — has often proven quite counter-productive. It not only cements young people into criminal vocations but also undermines the democratic values that are supposed to be the glue of social life.

This book examines responses to gangs, but its main focus is the context from which youth gangs arise. It considers the conditions that need to change for there to be any hope of overcoming young people's attractions to gang life. For youth gangs are a yell in the wilderness — a kind of perverted resistance to a world that is unequal and unfair. Youth, without any hope of a real future, will always be easy prey for gang recruiters looking for fresh cannon fodder.

Chapter 2
Gangs and Poverty

> Misery is when you heard on the radio that the neighborhood you live in is a slum but you always thought it was home.
>
> — Langston Hughes[1]

The debate about why young (mostly) males form and join street gangs is a long and contentious one. Social scientists and criminologists have spilled a great deal of ink debating the whys and wherefores. There is even an academic *Journal of Gang Research* (subscriptions $150 a year) dedicated to this and other gang-related topics[2] and a Street Gangs Book Club for which you can order the latest offerings online. Gangs have become not only a phenomena of the street but a minor industry rooted in university lecture halls and the growing number of gang specialists employed by law enforcement, social services and the private security industry.

The growth of street gangs can be traced to a series of push and pull factors. Push factors (those that drive people into a situation) include dysfunctional (often single-parent) families, family violence, marginalized (often immigrant or recently urbanized) communities, alienation (and expulsion) from schools, a lack of jobs or legal entrepreneurial opportunities, substance abuse at home, untreated mental health disorders and gang-involved relatives. Pull factors (those that attract people to a situation) involve first and foremost protection from violence on the streets. They also include the appeal of gang comradeship, the gang brand or identity, the chic of gang culture and access to guns and economic opportunities in the illegal economy, most notably through the transport and sale of drugs. Pull factors sometimes involve racial identity, as with much of the skinhead movement that reached its zenith in the 1990s. It organized around an anti-immigrant or white power focus in relatively homogeneous European societies such as Germany and Western Russia.

Where one puts the emphasis depends to a large degree on the philosophical and political preoccupations of the person doing the analyzing.

Delinquent Individuals

One school of thought is an updated version of the "bad seed" theory. James Q. Wilson and Stanton Samenow emphasize such notions as the "criminal mind," considering criminals to be the amoral "other" and downplaying the social and economic circumstances that push young people to gang life.[3] They tend to focus on the psychology of individual gang members and their moral failings, rejecting any notion of root causes such as poverty or inequality of opportunity. While avoiding overt racism, such views tend to assume a level playing field that discounts the situation of poor marginalized communities — be they Hispanic in Los Angeles, Bengali in Manchester, native in Edmonton, black in Rio or Muslim in Marseilles.

Because not all poor young people become gangsters it is assumed by these law-and-order champions that poverty is just an excuse that liberals fall back on for failing to get tough with youth gangs. They argue instead that children are "hardwired" at an early age by their genetic makeup or improper parenting. At the same time they maintain the somewhat contradictory stance that young gangsters have a choice, and that only severe penalties will dissuade them from making bad choices.

Wilson has gained kudos from the law-and-order crowd as the father of the "Broken Windows" theory of policing, which holds that the strict enforcement of minor crimes such as prostitution, littering, panhandling, graffiti and simple drug possession leads to crime-free neighborhoods. The Broken Windows school takes credit for New York City's reduced crime rate in the 1990s (a decade that also saw a massive increase in the NYC police budget), ignoring a similar drop in crime in other cities (San Francisco) that did not adopt such measures. George Kelling and Catherine Coles are Wilson acolytes whose work recommends throwing the book at young gang wannabes for minor offenses.[4]

Yet these kinds of "tough love" interventions (which are usually closer to "tough hate") have serious implications both for democracy and for integrating young people into respectful citizenship. They can also provide "at risk" youth with an excellent criminal education during their incarceration. In the end, the neoconservative pundits are less interested in reducing crime than in punishing the criminal. Unfortunately the "get tough" view has spread well beyond neoconservatism. It now resides across the political spectrum with liberals and even socialists jumping on board.

Most social scientists and criminologists who focus on gangs hold a more nuanced approach than Wilson and Samenow. But these two get a disproportionate public hearing because of media amplification of horrendous gang crimes and because politicians curry public favor by sounding off on crime issues.

Criminologist Marcus Felson in his 2006 study *Crime and Nature* develops a theory called the Big Gang Theory. Felson believes that the authorities inflate the reputations and capacities of gangs. It is in the interests of gangs to appear as violent and scary as possible, and they will mimic a larger, more dangerous gang (use of similar hand signals, tags, colors) in order to achieve this. Felson compares gangs to mimics in nature, such as the scarlet kingsnake that mimics the deadly coral snake in order to scare off predators.[5] The authorities, on the other hand, often inflate threats in order to toughen up legislation and sentencing while expanding their budget. The media frequently play along by portraying gangs as a monolithic out-of-control phenomena, using whatever trigger words are necessary to get public alarm bells ringing.

The street gang is an easy stereotype for pure villainy, whether in the media or in film. If you combine crime fear with prejudice against the particular group that is at the core of a gang (Hispanics, blacks, native peoples) you have a potent brew fermented for manipulation. For example, the Clint Eastwood movie *Gran Torino* (2008) pulls out a Hmong gang (the Hmong are from Laos) from the context of poverty and alienation in which it is rooted. Eastwood plays a retired curmudgeon who takes the side of his Lao neighbors who are being tormented by a Lao street gang. There is little sense of the whys and wherefores of the gang's existence or the social conditions that gave them birth. They are simply "the bad guys" in the usual Hollywood style.

Most people who have studied gangs closely or who have worked with them directly do not hold to the conservative approach of treating gangsters as examples of amoral individual "bad seeds." Not that they are against coming down on hard-core gang leaderships. But they tend to view gangs as a social phenomena and to differentiate between "at risk" youth and veteran gang leadership. They also tend to look at policy alternatives that start with the reality of gangs rather than their fantasy media image.[6]

Classic Gang Studies

Sociologist Frederic Thrasher's 1927 classic *The Gang* is still a seminal work in the field. Thrasher emphasized the importance of the context from which gangs arise. He identified the characteristic behavior of gangs as meeting face to face, milling, moving through space as a unit, conflict and planning. The result of this collective behavior is the development of tradition, unreflective internal structure, esprit de corps, solidarity, morale, group awareness, and attachment to a local territory.[7]

Chicago, where Thrasher worked, was the gang town par excellence of the early to mid-twentieth century. Although it continues to be a big gang town it has been replaced by Los Angeles as the world capital of youth gang culture.

In Thrasher's Chicago the gang habitat was marked by slums and poverty but also by immigration. Recently arrived immigrant communities provided some of the most fertile soil for gang activity. This is still true in societies marked by immigrant experience: North America, Australia and, increasingly, the more affluent countries of Western Europe.

But gangs are not just composed of immigrants — blacks and Hispanics have been in the US as long as people from white European stock. Indigenous people in Canada and New Zealand are participants in some of the most violent and unstable gangs. And while some of Thrasher's analysis linking youth gangs and slums is applicable to the gang-infested megacities of the Global South, few of these gangs come from external immigrant groups. They are more connected to indigenous and other local communities subject to long-term deprivation.

The annals of other classical gang studies — Cloward and Ohlin's *Delinquency and Opportunity* (1960) or the 1950s work of Walter Miller on the culture of the urban poor[8] — would have found the current focus on the delinquent individual gangster incomprehensible. But also incomprehensible would be what gangs have become today.

What has come to be known as the Chicago School regarded gangs as a temporary aberration — a sort of

If you take the Gini measurements of countries suffering major gang problems, you will find that they all rank as very unequal places. The US, with a Gini ranking of 40.0, is the most unequal of major countries in the North. It is also the one with the biggest problem of violent street gangs.

South Africa, with a rating of 57.8, is a major site of street and township gang activity. This is true of Papua New Guinea with 50.9, Guatemala with 55.1, Honduras with 53.8, El Salvador with 52.4 and Brazil with 57. Guatemala and Brazil are renowned for being two of the most unequal places on the globe. Haiti is virtually off the map with a rating of 59.2. Both Kenya and Nigeria, with serious gang issues, modify the situation slightly, registering in the low 40s because of more fluid social structures.

But the situation is clear. In societies where life choices are hemmed in by inequality and poverty but the young are exposed to the ostentatious wealth of the economic elite, the lure of gang life is strong. The logic is simple – why should they get it all and we be left out in the cold? In situations where movements for social justice and equality either do not exist or have stagnated, youth gangs often fill the vacuum.

failure of modernization that would be ironed out as the benefits of modern life trickled down to all. Gangs would disappear or have a reduced role when progress overcame inequality and discrimination. This of course has not happened and inequalities measured either domestically or internationally have become a permanent feature of market economies. Slums and the marginalized young (often defined in particular racial groups) are a permanent part of the social landscape. Today gangs are more deeply imbedded in poor communities than the classic gang theorists would have imagined possible.

Gangs and Immigration

Classic gang studies based at the University of Chicago analyzed young gangsters in the context of poverty (and racial and ethnic exclusion) shaped by immigration. The urban US of the late nineteenth and early twentieth centuries was the immigrant society par excellence with Polish, Irish, Jewish, Italian and later Hispanic gangs defending their turf and expressing their disillusionment with a mainstream society that discriminated against them. We can learn a lot from the immigration paradigm when we look at the more recent explosion of gang activity in Europe. European societies were relatively ethnically homogeneous until the arrival of "guest workers" in the 1970s. With the advent of globalization and an aging population, this flow of outside labor has grown into a flood.

The ethnic make-up varies, depending on the country involved. Some, such as France, Holland, Spain and the UK, have drawn both legal and illegal migrants from former colonies. Others, like Germany and the Scandinavian countries, have migrant populations from those countries bordering Europe, such as Turkey and Morocco. The fall of the Berlin Wall in late 1989 and the collapse of the Soviet Union the following year resulted in major movements of migrant populations — including a large number of Germans living in Russia who have now moved to Germany (1.6 million since 1989), although with little familiarity with German language and culture. Homogeneous European societies have found it difficult to cope with migrant populations, who are often subject to racial intolerance and discrimination.

This is a "perfect storm" for the development of street gangs. Second-generation migrant youth — North African in France, South Asian and Jamaican in the UK, Latin American in Spain and Turkish and Russian German in Germany — have become the core of gangs in response to conditions of cultural alienation and poverty. These gangs in turn have been met by gangs of youth of European descent organizing to defend "their" communities against the outsiders. Some of these latter gangs, which include skinheads, have connections to far-right, anti-immigrant political parties (the Front National in France, the British National Party, the National Democratic Party in Germany) who have a resurgence of support fueled by racism. Both sets of gangs have become involved in crime and the underground economy, although each tends to point the finger at the other as the main culprits. While gangs in Europe remain more sporadic and less rooted than gangs in the US, Central America and South Africa, they are a growing phenomena disturbing the good governance traditions of the European welfare states.

Surplus Population

For the first time in human history the majority of us live in cities — many in desperate conditions. Of the billion people designated very poor, over 750 million live in urban areas. Over the next three decades, urban growth will bring a further 2 billion people into cities in the Global South, doubling their size to about 4 billion people. These cities are already growing at a rate of about 70 million people per year.

In 2005 a billion people were living in urban slums, most of them squatters with an insecure grip on the edges of urban existence. The sheer number of these squatters is expected to double by the year 2030 to 2 billion. In cities such as Dhaka, Nairobi, Jakarta and São Paulo over a third of the population live in slums.[10]

Whether it's the shantytowns like *villa miseria* of Argentina or the Cité Soleil of Haiti, the potential for gang growth in major urban squatter settlements is alarming. When huge groups of the population have been abandoned to their "neighborhoods of exclusion" by official society, gang growth is highly likely, if not inevitable. The weakness of popular organizations (unions, community organizations, churches) also provides more room for gangsters. A world of slums becomes a world of gangs.

Desperate youth in search of meaning and a way out are drawn to gangs that seem to provide both. While the participation they offer is often shallow and dangerous there is not much else on offer. Take the Nairobi slum of Mathare, where some 500,000 people live in tin shacks with little or no contact with municipal services, including the police. This is the home of the famous "flying toilet." You do your business in a plastic bag and let it fly. Here people are regularly "taxed" by gangs such as the Mungiki, whose weapon of choice is the machete. It reached a point in 2006 where gangs sent residents fleeing into the streets as they tore apart their flimsy tin abodes to sell on the scrap metal market. Vigilante and police reprisals followed, catching many innocent people in a spiral of violence.[11]

But while gang horror stories are easy to trot out from almost any part of the globe, not all gangs are the same. For example, the four-hundred-odd *pandilla* gangs that haunt the poor areas of the Nicaraguan capital of Managua are sometimes seen as defenders of the local community. They also generate economic activity where there is precious little of it. The same can be said for Brazilian gangs, which often provide municipal services and even loans and mortgages to favela dwellers. In other words, gangs cannot be cut off so easily from the poor communities that gave them birth. Their families and friends live there, and they are part of the economic and cultural life of the place. In some communities where gangs are well established and of long duration (the favelas of urban Brazil, for example) they perform many of the tasks of a local government — policing, providing services, acting as a bank and sponsoring cultural activities like concerts and dances.

Anyone who claims to want to do something about suppressing youth gangs but refuses to deal with conditions of widespread poverty is fooling themselves and trying to fool us as well. A society that champions market-based success and get-rich-quick wealth while

Gang Girls

While the majority of youth gangs are made up of young males, females are also becoming members at an alarming rate. In the US estimates put female gang membership at around 10 percent, although it is higher in suburban, small city and rural gangs than in the more institutionalized gangs of the inner city. Estimates in Central America are much higher, ranging to 40 percent female membership – probably due to the lack of other employment opportunities and difficulty reintegrating into traditional family structures.

The appeal of gangs for young women is a combination of protection and family, which are often lacking in their destitute urban lives. It's a devil's bargain as the protection is heavily spiced with abuse and a major feature of their new "families" turns out to be exploitation. Young women in gangs are routinely subjected to sexual demands, including initiations where they must have sex with a number of male members. (There is little research on this, and some female gang members describe this initiation idea as a "male fantasy.")

Women are often expected to bring in gang income through prostitution and robbery. They usually play an auxiliary role for their male fellow gangsters, carrying weapons and drugs, recruiting new members or acting as decoys to lure the members of other gangs into a trap.

The story of Benky, a young woman in Guatemala City who has lived on the street since she was six, is not untypical. Benky's brother was killed by one Mara street gang so she joined the other for protection.

"It looked good from the outside," she says. "I thought I'd get the love I was missing. But they'd hit me. They ordered me around. They told me I had to rob someone or kill someone, and I did it."[12]

The Guatemala City gangs specialize in robbing buses, using teams that are 60 percent female for the task. The murder of bus drivers who resist extortion is a regular event in a country where 98 percent of murders go unsolved and the police are frequently allied with gangs.

Females maintain an uneasy balance between victimizer and victim, tipping mostly to the latter when they are part of male-dominated gangs. A study of Hispanic female gang members in Southern California found that nearly a third of them had suffered sexual abuse at home. Runaways from abuse or hopeless homes are looking for alternative forms of family and identity. But the new identity obtained by gang membership rarely escapes hierarchical male domination and exploitation.

· A rare alternative is all-female gangs such as the Spider Girls in Santiago, Chile, under-eighteen-year-olds who specialize in stealing jewelry in wealthy areas of the city. Studies of girls in US gangs indicate that only about 2 percent are from autonomous all-female gangs, which tend less toward criminal delinquency and more toward mutual support.

The idea of girl gangs tends to receive quite sensational press coverage. Particularly outrageous is the tabloid press in the United Kingdom. For example the *Daily Mail* ran a 2008 story entitled "The Feral Sex: The Terrifying Rise of Violent Girl Gangs."

A closer look at these kinds of stories reveal spontaneous acts of violence (very unladylike) but very little in the way of a sustained and institutionalized gang culture. But reports from the US, Germany and a number of other locations document an increase in the number of young women charged with violent crimes and the use of deadly weapons. This is not exactly the kind of equality envisioned by the feminist movement.

abandoning the poor deserves what it gets. And these days what it gets is young street gangs. As Canadian gang expert Michael Chettleburgh puts it in his study of Canadian gangs, "rather than recoiling from gangs, let's recoil from poverty, social exclusion, neglect of new immigrants, decaying cities, income disparity, 'affluenza' and the other social afflictions that drive youth to gangs in the first place."[13]

While the Canadian situation differs radically from the situation in Brazil or Nigeria or France the starting point needs to be the same. You can't tackle a gang problem without tackling a poverty problem, an opportunity problem, a discrimination problem, a corruption problem, an inequality problem. Violent youth gangs must be held accountable but they must also be recognized for what they often are — a symptom of a social system where the young poor are no longer willing to shrug helplessly and accept a life where the dice are loaded against them.

Chapter 3
The Underground Economy

It's a war out here, man. I mean everyday strug-
gling to survive, so you know we just do what we
can. We ain't got no choice, and if that means getting killed, well s___, that's what n_____ do around
here to feed their families.[1]

It's always been difficult for the young to break into the
labor market. Employers want experience and a proven
track record indicating trustworthiness. Anyone who
has tried to get employment to either help pay for their
schooling or because they have left school is familiar with
the phenomena of the "Mcjob" — low pay and long hours
for young workers in the service sector. Add to this an
overall job crisis, which is bad enough for young Muslims in the poor areas of Berlin or Marseilles or young
Hispanics in Chicago and LA, but catastrophic for those
growing up in the sprawling shantytowns of the Global
South or the young of the post-Communist world.

In the urban outskirts of French cities (known as the
zones grises, or gray zones, for their monotonous derelict

The Changing Face of Work

It has become a cliché that how we work and how we think about work is changing. The old certainties of secure industrial employment in the affluent societies and the relatively stable agricultural employment in the South are disappearing. Both have been ripped up by the shift of industrial production to low-wage unregulated countries, particularly China, and the flooding of poor economies with cheap foodstuffs from the corporate estates run by global agribusiness.

The decline of these two types of employment has left workers, particularly those just entering the labor market, in a difficult situation. Downward pressure on wages is shaping a race to the bottom in both rich and poor worlds. The watchwords of the new work world are "flexibilization," "outsourcing" and "casualization." The result is poorer paid jobs where workers have lost many of their employment benefits and often work longer hours for less income. Cutbacks that took off in the 1980s Thatcher/Reagan revolution mean that workers have lost much of the safety net that used to support low-income people and carry them through periods of unemployment. In the old industrial world, once-stable working-class communities have become impoverished and destabilized.

This has hit those just entering the workforce particularly hard. Low-paid service jobs (in the retail trades such as fast food) often mean long hours

public housing landscape) many conventional stores have closed. They are replaced by the occasional black market mini-mart that sells stolen goods at knockdown prices. In the former Red Belt surrounding Paris (where the Communist Party was once strong) or the les Biscottes area of Lille, drug trafficking, vandalism and confrontations with the police are the stuff of daily life for many adolescents (by no means all of them migrants from Africa).

and working at more than one job to make ends meet. In France new forms of flexible work contracts established in 2006 make it much easier to dismiss young workers. The situation is similar all over Europe, with young workers vulnerable to the "last hired, first fired" syndrome. Fully one-third of Spaniards under the age of twenty-four are without work. Other EU countries that have youth unemployment rates of over 25 percent include France, Italy and Ireland. It is worse in the US (particularly for visible minorities), where the trade union movement is weak and workers' rights are less well established. The psychological effects of both unemployment and underemployment can have a devastating effect. Robbed of their traditional identity as breadwinners, young men, in particular, are often easy prey to the violent predatory self-image of macho violence promoted in gangsta culture.

In the Global South the situation is complicated. While many countries (particularly in Asia) have gained industrial employment (albeit at low wages in hazardous conditions), millions of people who are unable to support themselves in the countryside are flooding the cities looking for jobs. There are not enough of these jobs to go around, and many end up living in squatter communities and existing on the margins of the mainstream economy. Here too, youth unemployment and underemployment provide fertile ground for street gang culture.

It's not easy being young; it's even harder being young and poor.

While young people under twenty-five make up only one-quarter of the working population, they make up 47 percent of the unemployed worldwide. It's even worse if you just measure the Global South, with a young population, where young people are 3.8 times more likely to be unemployed than older workers.[2] This is further aggravated by the fact that the youth job market is unstable, with poorly paid temporary or part-time jobs. The situation is of course worse, much worse, for the millions of kids who grow up in squatter settlements.

Just because these kids don't have jobs doesn't mean they don't work. Girls in particular (for whom education is often considered a luxury) work long hours both inside and outside the home. Nepalese and Bangladeshi girls of 10 years of age work up to 10 hours a day. Ethiopian 10-year-old girls often put in a 14- to 16-hour day. And it's not just girls. In HIV-ravaged Uganda 34 percent of young men living in slums head a household (only 5 percent in non-slum areas).[3]

In the Global South childhood as we know it in the West is enjoyed by a shrinking minority. Poor families need their children to contribute to the family coffers. They must earn in whatever way they can, and with stable jobs so hard to come by, this sometimes means by illegal activity. In Southeast Asia poor village girls often become prostitutes in order to support their parents. Many have little choice as they are sold into a life of prostitution by desperate parents in places like Burma (Myanmar) or the poor rural areas of Thailand.

Sea of Illegality
The underground economy is not caused by gangs but it is the sea they swim in. The informal sector of repair shops, scavenging, loan sharks, prostitution, home manufacturing, street selling, begging, fencing, catering, hair

styling, driving illegal cabs, fortune-telling, writing official and unofficial letters — any manner of "service" that people can find a market for — is how most poor people survive. Gangs often try and find a way to "tax" such activities, offering a form of "protection" in exchange for being able to carry on marginal businesses. In other words, pay up or else. Some gangs will even extend loans to such enterprises, helping to consolidate their control over the economy of a poor community.

The underground economy — or the informal sector as economists call it — is sometimes lionized for its economic efficiency. Peruvian economist Hernando de Soto is perhaps the highest-profile advocate of the informal enterprise and the legalization of squatter housing as a potential engine to tackle poverty. The boom in NGO-sponsored microcredit (i.e., the provision of small loans to poor people to enable them to start up a small business or improve their housing) results from the recognition that many in the Global South depend on the underground economy for their daily bread. Still, in a global economy structured to enrich and empower the corporate elite it is hard to imagine much effective competition coming from shantytowns. Moreover the informal sector is almost always precarious and the activities carried out sometimes illegal and dangerous. While it comes close to dominating economic life in many parts of the urban South, it also exists in a more marginal way in poor communities in North America and Europe. In cities like Montreal and Manchester poor people engage

The War on Drugs

The first modern attempts to prohibit the use of narcotics date back to 1909 and the International Opium Commission set up in Shanghai to prevent the British from flooding China with opium. The war on drugs gathered pace under the influence of J. Edgar Hoover and the FBI in the 1930s and was made a major priority of the Nixon and then Reagan Republican presidencies. Its big supporters are prohibitionist countries like the US and Sweden as well as UN agencies such as the Vienna-based UN Office on Drugs Control and Crime, and the International Narcotics Board. Conservative and fundamentalist religious influence has also been a factor in sustaining the drug prohibition campaign.

The attempt to stamp out widespread drug consumption has turned out to be an expensive fantasy. This war-without-end soaks up about $40 billion a year in the US and the same amount in the European Union. The US has jailed millions of people (mostly black and Hispanic and poor) for their roles in the drug supply line. Simple possession of relatively harmless recreational drugs such as marijuana can net serious jail time. Take the case of the Young family in Mississippi, who got decades-long sentences, or John Avery, serving 20 years in Kentucky, or Scott Walt, who got 24 years in California. James Geddes of Oklahoma was sentenced to 95 years in prison for possession of 5 marijuana plants in 1993. The sentence was reduced to 90 years (he ended up serving 11).

The Washington-based Pew Center in its 2009 report on American prisons states that "sentencing and release laws passed in the 1980s and 1990s put so many more people behind bars that last year the incarcerated population reached 2.3 million and, for the first time, one in 100 adults was in prison or jail."[4]

This rate of incarceration makes the US (with Russia) one of the most punitive countries in the world. A majority of prisoners (55.1 percent) are jailed for drug offenses.

The UK-based group Transform estimates that the UK is wasting around $6 billion every year on a drug war that achieves the opposite of its stated aims, while simultaneously maximizing the harm associated with drug use and creating almost $14 billion in crime costs.[5]

Internationally, the War on Drugs is an even bigger failure. Over $6 billion has been spent on Plan Colombia to diminish the cocaine supply at source, with few noticeable results. A drug cartel figure, Mexico's Joaquin "El Chapo" Guzman, made it onto *Forbes* magazine's list of billionaires in 2009. The Colombian cocaine lord Pablo Escobar made it in 1993. Mexico and Central America are being torn apart as thousands are killed every year in drug wars and in futile attempts to create a pristine, drug-free world. The poor states of West Africa have become the latest victims as the drug cartels seek new passageways to get cocaine to industrial world markets. Across the world in Afghanistan, the US and its NATO allies refuse to buy up the crops of opium farmers (for painkillers and a range of other uses) and instead launch eradication campaigns, driving them into the arms of the Taliban. Poor southern farmers who are encouraged to grow drug crops receive very little for their efforts and live in a situation of perpetual insecurity.

Prohibitionist evangelism coordinated by the UN Commission on Narcotic Drugs amounts to a lot of wheel-spinning. The result of making drugs illegal is a massive criminal infrastructure, a wave of corruption of police and other public employees, and economic oxygen that keeps street gangs powerful and dangerous at the lower end of drug retail sales.

Some drugs are harmful, some less so, some hardly at all. But by making all drugs illegal the prohibitionists have spread the harm far beyond the user. They have poisoned society with corruption and criminality and created a vast shadow economy based on fear and violence. This shadow economy has spread its tentacles into almost every part of the world.

Meanwhile the demand for drugs has barely slackened. Addicts have become criminals. Treatment is hard to come by. Significant tax revenues on the sale of regulated drugs elude capture – such revenues could be used to support the public health costs associated with drug abuse. Drugs have escaped public regulation and quality control. Resources squandered on the drug war are not available for healthy development that could provide economic alternatives to the drug trade. In too many cities, in continent after continent, street gangs of violent and angry young men are the local evidence of the failure of drug prohibition.

in the informal economy as a way of supplementing the minimal social provisions provided by the state. It is in this larger informal sector that gang economics is constructed.

The sex trade, muggings, house robberies, fraud, extortion and protection rackets, and "express kidnappings" (you grab someone with an ATM card and force them to drain their accounts) have all become part of the economic arsenal of street entrepreneurs. But far and away the biggest source of income for most street gangs is the drug trade. Estimates are largely guesswork but the global trade in illegal drugs is reckoned to be hundreds of billions of dollars.

The drug trade is the oxygen of the street gang economy, causing street gangs to multiply and expand dramatically. In North America this dates particularly from the widespread availability of relatively cheap crack cocaine in the 1980s. In the Global South (especially Central America) the major expansion has been fueled by the US-inspired War on Drugs (see box). Gangs act both as conduits to smuggle drugs to North America (through Mexico, Central America and the Caribbean) or Europe (through West Africa) or are involved in local distribution. But it would be a mistake to imagine that such gangs "run" the drug trade. Rather they provide the pathway for the cocaine economy centered in Andean Latin America (Colombia in particular).

The overall drug economy is controlled by adult drug cartels that employ the gangs at fairly minimal cost to carry out local operations. Drug trade profits are very unevenly distributed, with gang leaders enjoying a differential in income over street dealers, couriers and foot soldiers that is reminiscent of that between corporate CEOs and factory workers and bank tellers. Some of the more "talented" of these leaders provide a recruiting pool for adult drug cartels and may go onto a successful adult career in crime.

Gang Economics

A close study of the political economy of a US street gang in a 2000 issue of the *Quarterly Journal of Economics* reveals just how the benefits are spread. The gang is identified as African American and highly successful, but both its name and the city in which it operates have been suppressed to protect sources. The average take for a street-level foot soldier is less than the hourly US minimum wage. Most foot soldiers also maintain low-level jobs in the legitimate economy to maintain a semi-livable income. The income of the gang leaders is ten to twenty times higher than that of the average foot soldier. The study estimates that the gang leader takes home between $4,200 and $10,900 a month, for a yearly income in the $50,000 to $130,000 range. The situation is complicated by such factors as police crackdowns and inter-gang warfare, which in this case increased dramatically with the opening of the crack cocaine market. During the drug wars the gang was forced to either hire relatively expensive warriors (at $2000 a month) or increase the amount paid to foot soldiers because of increased risk or to maintain their loyalty. Families of those who die in action are due bereavement and compensation payments of $5000 because "you've got to respect family."[6]

Not only is the work with street gangs badly paid, it is also extremely dangerous. Over the four years of the life of the gang in the study, members involved for all four years faced a 25 percent chance of being killed as part of their gang activity.

The average death rate for African Americans 14 to 17 years of age is 1 in 1000 a year; if they join the gang it is 1 in 80. This does not include the number of serious injuries or arrests and convictions that are a big part of gang life (6 arrests and 2 non-fatal injuries per member over the 4 years). By any objective standard this does not seem a particularly attractive form of employment. So why do these young men continue to be involved with drug gangs?

Part of the answer can be traced to a lack of attractive economic opportunities in the conventional job market. Another may be the attraction of the media-inspired notion of a glamorous "gangsta" lifestyle. This is similar to the hope of some in the conventional economy that they can move from rags to riches, part of the glue that helps maintain the work ethic of the corporate-dominated market economy. In the underground gang economy this belief is also the source of increased violence as young foot soldiers try to gain a reputation as potential leadership material. Overall the drug economy needs to be maintained by the use of violence because this is the only way gangs can guard or expand their sales territory and keep individual gang members and customers in line. If drugs were decriminalized such issues would fall under the laws that govern normal commercial practice. But illegality means gangs and violence.

The small economic rewards most members glean from gang life mean that the attractions of this dangerous engagement must be about more than the money you can make peddling drugs on the street corner. A sense of belonging, the appeal of a culture, the ability to attract the opposite sex, a romantic self-image, a lack of alternatives, an outlet for frustration and alienation may all be much more important than economic rewards at the bottom of the gang ladder.

How representative is the profile of the US gang to street gangs elsewhere in the world? It cannot be stressed too much that street gangs vary dramatically from country to country and from community to community. Each community needs to look at its own gang problem and understand local gang history, what attracts kids to gangs in that community and how deeply rooted the street gangs are. However, there are some parallels. Almost everywhere, well-established gangs are hierarchical, with those at the top benefiting from the low-paid and risky activity of those at the bottom. In this way the street gang mirrors the structure of more "respectable" forms of business organization.

Institutionalized Gangs

The context in which a street gang evolves gives either greater or lesser scope for the gang's activities. In the slums of cities like Rio or Nairobi, where vast areas are neglected, municipal services are either rudimentary or completely absent and police move about in large groups (if at all), the possibilities for profitable street gang growth are much greater. There gangs can translate their economic power into a kind of quasi-political power. This role provides a diverse stream of income, including taxes, interest income from credit and mortgages, fines and sometimes control of services such as water and electricity. Such gangs may still be involved in robbery, kidnapping and other forms of extortion, but these are mostly carried out beyond gang territory.

Inside their territory, gangs such as Rio's Comando Vermelho (Red Command) maintain a strict regime of law and order, including a system of criminal justice and punishment. If a gang member is caught stealing, he is badly beaten for a first offense, shot in both hands for a second and executed for a third. A similar regime is run by Rio's other two main gangs, Terceiro Comando Puro (TCP, Pure Third Command) and Amigos dos Amigos (ADA, Friends of Friends), or São Paulo's notorious Primeiro Comando da Capital (PCC, First Capital Command). Together the Rio gangs influence territory where nearly 30 percent of the city's 6 million people live. They are a part of everyday life. Comando Vermelho even promotes, produces and sells Brazilian funk music, sponsoring concerts every Sunday.[7]

The gangs of Rio have morphed into something quite different from Cincinnati's North Side Taliban or Toronto's Malvern Crew. Youth gangs in the wealthier countries of the North have neither the opportunity nor the ambition to play such a role. While the street soldiers of Comando Vermelho may not earn as much of a living as North American street gang rank-and-file, their leaders have become major players in the criminal underworld and in municipal politics. As a result they tend to be older, hanging on well after gang members in other areas have left the life behind (usually around the age of twenty-eight).

The other gangs much feared by law enforcement are the Salvadoran Maras. They seem particularly threatening with their heavily tattooed faces and bodies. Some view these gangs as transnational threats because they operate both in North and Central America. However, most people familiar with youth gangs debunk the notion that they are centralized, highly efficient crime networks. Instead they see gang members as either migrating or local gangs picking up on the fearsome reputation of these gangs to gain local "street cred." Gang members may move around and have gang contacts in other places but the direction of gang activity and the shape of gang organization are primarily local. While they are not centralized international crime syndicates like the Mafia, they do take advantage of their contacts to help move weapons, drugs and people (mostly innocent migrants) from South to North and back again.[8]

Writing about the gang-ridden Cape Flats region of South Africa, criminologist Andre Standing concludes that operating without formal regulation, the illicit economy displays the most vivid failings of free market enterprise, what we may refer to as "predatory capitalism." Most strikingly, the spoils of crime are concentrated among a tiny minority, some of whom have become multi-millionaires. Predatory capitalism allows winners to take all.[9]

Standing adds that the capital (money) accumulated, instead of trickling down and improving the situation of the poor people in the communities in the Cape Flats, "is in fact pumped out of the area."[10]

Elsewhere gangs also capitalize on local opportunities but show the same pattern of Standing's predatory capitalism. Kenya's infamous Mungiki Gang is heavily involved in extortion rackets in the lucrative minibus taxi industry. In Phuket City in Thailand youth gangs specialize in bicycle theft. In the Congo and West Africa child soldiers are recruited to smuggle diamonds or precious metals. Zhu Lien Bang (the United Bamboo Gang) of Taiwan specializes in weapons and human smuggling as well as the heroin trade.

But whatever the economic lure, young gang members take great risks for very little gain. In addition to low wages, most gang members pay regular dues. If there is any money to be made, it flows upwards to a slightly older gang leader or an adult criminal who may be a local warlord or part of a drug cartel or an urban crime set-up.

Any solid economic opportunity could easily provide a pole of attraction away from the dubious opportunities offered the gang foot soldier by the underground economy.

Chapter 4
Gangs and Their Communities

> The kids are like a nervous wreck. Because like my grandkids, with all this shooting and stuff, they jump; they're nervous in their sleep…so you can imagine how the little babies are around here.
> — Shirlene, who is raising two grandchildren in a housing project in a US city.[1]

Most youth or street gangs are rooted in a particular geographic community that they count on for support or at least acquiescence so that they can maintain their operations. This is obtained in a number of ways — fear and violence, peace-keeping and conflict resolution, preventing crimes by outsiders, giving to charity, providing jobs to community members and advocating for rights with officialdom. Some gangs support politicians.

The relationship between a gang and a community depends on a number of factors — the strength of police or another official presence, the ethnic makeup of the community, its poverty level, the nature of the local economy and local rates of drug consumption.

The gang's institutional roots are key both to how they operate and how difficult it is for a community to deal with them. Many youth gangs, particularly in industrial societies, come and go from smaller cities and towns with little notice. There is also an ebb and flow to gang members. In Rochester, New York — a de-industrialized city and a heavy gang town — 50 percent of gang members stayed in gangs less than a year. Members who grow out of their gangs leave, mostly with few problems, despite myths to the contrary.[2] In the urban shantytowns of the Global South, where gangs are more rooted and economic opportunities scarce, gang membership is often of longer duration.

Communities with gang problems look a lot different depending on where they are. In the cities of Europe and North America the gang habitat is frequently low-income, high-rise "projects" that are publicly subsidized housing. These often soulless developments lack the streetscape and eyes-on-the-street necessary for local residents to engage in self-policing or working with existing police forces. A sense of community is difficult to sustain as neighbors tend to live a privatized existence in isolated units. Anonymity gives cover to gang activities. Public spaces go unclaimed and are often left to garbage and neglect. Elevators are prone to accident and breakdown. Stairwells and underground garages and laundry rooms and anonymous entrances and corridors leave ample hang-out spaces for gangs to sell drugs or exercise control by intimidating residents.

Modern US youth gang culture arguably has its roots in the Chicago projects.

In France gangs of youth from the North African and Caribbean communities fought with police in the projects of the *banlieues* surrounding Paris in the fall of 2005. The riots started in the high-rise suburb of Clichy-sous-Bois and spread throughout the country over the next twenty nights. When it was all over 9000 cars had been burned and nearly 3000 youths arrested, putting an end to the myth of French republican equality and testifying to the alienation of youth shut up in suburban slums around the country.

In many cases a community (often represented by the mothers of that community) reaches a precarious negotiated order with a gang. Younger gang members are more easily tolerated than older ones. But this informal negotiation is inherently unstable and breaks down whenever there is an increase in violence. In the US, public policy that discourages and penalizes welfare dependence often drives single mothers into dead-end jobs for mere survival. The mothers are caught in the impossible situation of leaving their children at home in whatever inadequate child-care situation they can arrange. Many choose to withdraw from employment altogether (despite the economic penalties) rather than leave their kids in harm's way.[3]

The habitats of gangs in Africa and Latin America are usually low-rise squatter settlements, with the tin shack the predominant building form. Although in some Latin American cities, like Rio and Caracas, the high-rise urban form—although not in the context of huge public housing developments—also dominates. The settlements in much of the Global South often perch precariously on hillsides or are jammed in beside railways or in diseased swamplands. The squatters are in a situation of vulnerability in every sense—they have no legal rights to their dwellings and the dwellings are themselves unsafe. For the most part they lack dependable employment. They are vulnerable to illness and disease because of poor living conditions, bad water, non-existent sanitation and few medical facilities. They are vulnerable to the whims of both civic authorities and the police. They may be evicted if the land they are living on is desired for a more profitable purpose or if they are from the wrong ethnic group.

Is it any wonder that their kids join gangs as both a protection and a form of identity? Then the communities become vulnerable to gangs who claim to protect and advocate for them but often at a terrible price. This is the setting in which most of the gangs in the Global South operate.

The Flats

For poor communities gangs are a lose-lose situation. Already in a precarious economic and political situation, the gangs take away the potential power of communities to organize themselves either for economic self-help or to gain political traction with the local state. With gangs major players in a community, other forms of political organization are either squeezed for space or corrupted by making deals with gang leaders.

Gangs are neither the product nor the cause of corruption — they are both. Take the hundreds of gangs that dominate the massive Cape Flats shantytown outside of the glamorous confines of commercial Cape Town in South Africa. Gang membership is estimated between 60,000 and 100,000 members. The big gang names are legend — the Americans and the Hard Livings are dominant, but there are also the Sexy Boys, the School Boys and the Junky Funky Kids — their names and reputations known in even the remotest rural areas of South Africa.

Since the end of apartheid, gangs have fed on the disappointment of poor and black South Africans over the course of the Mbeki and now Zuma African National Congress government of "business-as-usual." Expectations of significant change in the wrenching inequality that characterized the apartheid era have been badly shaken.

The ANC governments have been largely absent from the sprawling and crime-ridden flats. Unemployment is over 40 percent, with unemployment for those under thirty a staggering 61 percent. The gangs have monopolized much of the economic opportunity through a combination of drug-dealing and extortion. Inter-gang violence has taken dozens of lives. In the late 1990s surveys carried out among Flats citizens recorded a widespread belief in police corruption and shielding of gang members, notably members of the Hard Livings.[4] By 2006 an all-out gang war had broken out in the Western Cape over who would control the lucrative crystal meth market that was reportedly being supplied by Chinese triads (a centuries-old criminal organization) and Nigerian gangs.

The experience of gang violence is an everyday affair. According to the local newspaper, the *Cape Argus*, 97 percent of children surveyed reported hearing gunshots, nearly half had seen the dead body of a stranger and nearly as many the dead body of a relative or somebody they knew who had died from unnatural causes. According to a teacher, Mrs. Bester, from a Cape Flats school system, "Many times it is children that were in your class that is now a gangster. Then you feel as if you wasted your time because in actual fact you are raising gangsters."[5]

In 1996 some citizens decided to take the law into their own hands and formed the Islamic-oriented People Against Gangsterism and Drugs (PAGAD), which has reportedly been involved in a number of extra-legal killings of gang leaders. PAGAD is also suspected in a series of terrorist bombings of Cape Town Jewish, gay and secular targets.[6]

But Cape Flats is more than this. It has a vital culture, a lively music scene and many grassroots initiatives where citizens try and move beyond mere survival. Nor are the street gangs simply a criminal blight opposed by the mainstream community. According to criminologist Andre Standing, there is "considerable support for criminals who are elsewhere despised and feared." He adds,

Support for criminals may only be evident by a willingness to "turn a blind eye"… residents provide deliberate misinformation to investigating officers…it may be the case that what seems to be community toleration stems from community intimidation — residents are too scared to speak out because they fear reprisal.[7]

But Standing concludes that there are numerous times when community support for gang activities is "explicit and active." Gangs in the Flats are some of the main employers, particularly of the young, in such areas as the drug economy and illegal drinking establishments. Gang leaders who become wealthy often invest (i.e., launder) their money in more legitimate enterprises that provide local communities with money and jobs — although frequently such investments are made outside the community. But whether the jobs are legal or illegal, as one of Standing's interviewees put it, "you cannot expect families to ask too many questions when food is put on the table."[8] So institutionalized gangs like the Americans and the Hard Livings have, like it or not, become important economic and political players in the Cape Flats.

Links to the Adult World
The case of the Cape Flats shows that youth gangs are not out there on their own but must fit into an adult world and deal with adults. The drug cartels that supply gangs are mostly adults, and so are the police who may

be their enemies. Their friends, their aiders and abettors and their families are made up at least partially of adults, the community leaders (often mothers and grandmothers) are adults, as are the business and political elites that control access to resources.

The more institutionalized the gang, the greater the importance that these adult connections assume. This is less true for the youth street gangs of Europe and North America, where gang membership and even the existence of gangs tend to wax and wane. In smaller communities and suburbs such gangs are more peer group undertakings — signs of temporary revolt organized around a particular cause or venture and without an enduring history in their communities.

The institutionalized gang is likely to take hold in situations where official society ignores or neglects significant parts of the population (particularly the young population). Economic policy is geared to the needs of the well-off or to earn foreign. exchange to buy goods abroad or to pay off a country's debts. In such circumstances the youth gang is one of the symptoms of neglect.

It is not surprising that communities have an ambivalent attitude toward gangs. Gang members are often their own children. There is sometimes an economic stake in gang activities. The relationship between street gangs and their communities tends to become tense and strained when there is too much violence or the gang is seen as particularly arbitrary or unpredictable. Otherwise it's a question of adaptation and live and let live.

The leadership of the gangs often sees the gang as a parallel and similar institution to what they see in official adult society. "I am just a businessman really"; "the police are really just another kind of gang"; "politicians do it, so why pick on us?"; "we are just fighting to protect the community" are the justifications gang leaders resort to. When interviewed by *New Yorker* reporter Jon Lee Anderson, Rio gang leader Fernandinho (of the Pure Third Command) compared his function to that of a local mayor.[9]

Such responses may be self-serving but they have the ring of truth. They reflect the attitudes of those who live in hyperghettos and shantytowns that the power and wealth accumulated by the politicians and police who either exploit or ignore them is illegitimate. And who is to say they are wrong? They often live in a political and economic culture fraught with corruption, get-rich-quick schemes, the manipulation of public power to enhance individual wealth, and the general triumph of greed, inequality and unfairness. To change such perceptions it is necessary to start addressing the bleak realities that lie behind them.

White Racist Gangs

One of the myths surrounding street gangs, particularly in North America, is that they are inevitably made up of minorities of color – black, Latino, Asian or native (particularly in the Canadian West). In fact, many North American gang members are white – ranging from 10 percent in the US to 18 percent in Canada.[10] Most are involved in regular street gangs but a few make up the core of the white racist gang movement. These are youth gangs that organize around racial identity and are among the most violent and unpredictable of all.

Conditions of joblessness and the collapse of economic security have fueled the growth of these racist gangs. They can be seen as a reaction to an increasingly globalized economy that has displaced old privileges and status, transferring jobs overseas and drawing in a diversity of workers from other countries and cultures. Racist gangs see the white race as under siege and in danger of being displaced from its dominant role.

Many of these young gangsters identify with the skinhead movement that had its origins in the UK in the late 1960s. While the first wave of skinheads were not racist, a second wave in the 1970s took on an aggressive racist stance to defend all things British against foreigners.

Racist gangs have been on the rise in Europe since waves of immigration starting in the 1970s challenged the traditional ethnic makeup of what were relatively homogeneous societies. In Europe racist gangs are frequently associated with football hooliganism. They are prone to attack not only opposition supporters but anyone they regard as different: the immigrant "other," people of color, Roma ("gypsies"), Jews, gay people. Heavy drinking and spasms of random violence characterize these groups.

In Germany, after the fall of the Berlin Wall, the skinhead and other racist youth movements gained momentum, particularly in the eastern part of the country. The social conditions of inequality and disappointment (over the lack of personal opportunity in post-Communism) helped fuel this upsurge. The movement was marked by the usual exaggerated masculinity and subcultural style of clothing, tattoos and music. German national pride was (to a degree) rekindled by unification. The use of Nazi symbolism proved an important attention-getter in a Germany sensitive to its recent history. The movement has gone into relative decline, replaced by a lower-key youth gang racism that is less likely to aggressively flaunt a neo-Nazi identity.

It is in Russia that racist youth gangs (mostly skinheads) remain the most dangerous force. Some estimates run as high as 50,000 racist and skinhead youth. Every year these gangs kill dozens of migrants, mostly from the Asian and Caucasus regions of the country but occasionally visiting foreigners as well. A group of skinheads in Moscow was convicted of murder and attempted murder of twenty Central Asians. At trial they claimed that they had committed the attacks in order to "cleanse Russian blood." In April 2010 the judge who presided over the trial was murdered gangland style in St. Petersburg. Russian skinheads tap into a xenophobia that has gripped the country due to economic insecurity. There are suspicions that racist youth are involved with both organized crime and sections of the security services. In addition to racial assaults, deadly attacks have been launched against anti-fascist and other democratic activists, many of whom have been killed.

Southern California is the home of two of the most racist violent gangs in the US – Public Enemy No 1 (PEN1) and the Nazi Lowriders. These gangs organize around the notion of "white pride" and attack blacks and Latinos. Again it is the Los Angeles area that pops up as "gang central" – a home of some uneasy housemates – neo-Nazis along with black (the Crips and the Bloods) and Latino gangs (the Maras).

US racist gangs have their roots in the Ku Klux Klan but more recently are connected to the Aryan Brotherhood (aka the Firm) – a violent white prison gang that started up in the 1960s. The Brotherhood was created by Irish bikers in California's maximum security San Quentin prison. Much of the original Brotherhood leadership has been broken up by racketeering charges. Today the Brotherhood's identity is blurred with a plethora of other white gangs, drawing particularly from the young racist skinhead movement (there are also anti-racist skinheads). The US racist gang movement is influenced by white supremacist propagandists like the virulent California-based Tom Metzger.

Despite their celebration of racial purity, such gangs draw their culture from many places – Norse myths, Celtic crosses, English Doc Martens boots, Confederate flags, Lonsdale and Pitbull clothing. The racist gang movement also has its own music, a punk and heavy metal blend, featuring groups like Skrewdriver and Extreme Hatred.

These "white or ethnic pride" groupings attack not just for reasons of profit and turf but as a means of racial purification. They overlap with football hooligans and use the venue of football games or post-games to terrorize their targets. Such football gangs tend to refer to themselves as a "crew" or "firm" and their chosen names denote a martial and racial self-image – Gladiator's Firm (Russia), White Pride (Denmark), Psycho Fans and Destroyers (Poland). They frequently target ethnic groups that are national scapegoats. In Israel the football gang La Familia picks on Palestinians; in Russia football gangsters reserve their wrath for Asian Russians or those from the Caucasus. In the UK it's the "Pakis." Although they provide a recruiting ground for racist movements, the majority of young people involved in football gangs grow out of them by their mid-twenties.

Chapter 5
Gang Appeal

Fear and desire to have a reputation on the streets made me do it. When I got into the streets, I saw the glamour of it. I wanted a reputation there. What better way to get a reputation than to pick up a pistol? I've shot several people.

—A Colorado gang member[1]

Young (mostly) men join gangs for a lot of reasons—not all of them to do with poverty and a lack of economic opportunity. One of the draws of a gang is the identity it provides for those who have grown up in vulnerable circumstances without a strong sense of self. Other contributing factors are dysfunctional families and a community with weak religious, political and social institutions, leading to a lack of moral bearings in the world.

Gangs provide a model of masculine empowerment in situations where other models are either absent or appear invalid. Fragile egos are prone to dramatic overstatement in all kinds of hyper-masculine behaviors. This is where the culture of respect and the ultimate crime of "dissing" (showing disrespect) come in. As a gang member incarcerated in a Colorado prison put it:

> Violence starts to escalate once you start to disrespect me. Once you start to second guess my manhood, I'll fuck you up. You start coming at me with threats, then I feel offended. Once I feel offended I react violently. That's how I was taught to react.[2]

American criminologist Deanna Wilkinson believes that crafting a powerful social identity is a critical tool for survival in the inner-city context.[3] Over 41 percent of the violent shootings she studied were caused by conflicts over "identity/status." Any survey of gang members will tell much the same story. Dissing — which can involve anything from incurring drug debts to looking the wrong way at a girlfriend — can be a capital offense in a gang.

Against this background of fragile male egos and violence, a permission-giving culture has grown up to justify trigger-finger machismo. Gang culture has spread outwards mostly from the United States and now exerts an influence almost everywhere street gangs exist. It draws youth into a kind of pseudo-family with its own history of triumph and tragedy, its own rules and its own signifiers.

Gang Culture Goes Global
Gang culture is by now familiar, especially in its superficialities. It involves a way of dressing — loose-fitting

Tattoos

> We like to have tattoos of monks because like us they live in the darkness, don't sleep, dress in black and use hoods that cover their faces. Just like us.
>
> – Arce, a gang member from the Reparto Schick district of Managua, Nicaragua[4]

Like secret societies or religious sects of old, youth gangs have an elaborate range of tattoos to celebrate their identities and communicate with the outside world. Nicaraguan *pandillas* use an array of images, including clowns, crowns of thorns, pierced hearts and dragons. The details of a tattoo are worked out between the gang member and the tattoo artist to celebrate a killing, a passage in life, a broken romance or a significant death or grief.

Tattoos are a way of sending a message. The message may be a warning to other gangs. It may be a demand for respect from the local community. It may be a sexual come-on to women. It may be a celebration of comradeship with fellow gang members. It may be a slap in the face to respectable society.

baggy pants, baseball caps, expensive athletic shoes and other professional sports paraphernalia such as jogging gear or team jackets, as well as gaudy jewelry such as gold chains that have come to be known as "bling."

Another element of a gang uniform is the color, which acts as an identifier for particular gangs. The Los Angeles gangs, the Bloods and the Crips, are identified with red and blue, respectively. Colors also help to indicate the kind of "turf" on which it is appropriate for a gang member to wander. It is not a good idea to be on one gang's territory wearing the colors of an opposing gang.

In the poor countries of the Global South (Brazil,

The impetus for tattooing (like many other aspects of gang life) comes at least partially from the US, where gang members imprisoned in California used tattoos extensively.

Tattoos have become a broader fashion statement among middle-class youth. The difference is the type of the tattoo (gang tattoos are frequently violent or threatening) and its location. Fashion tattoos are often discreet and hidden by clothing, while gang tattoos are literally in your face and cover extensive visible parts of the body.

A tattoo can become a social stigma that marks your life long after you have left the gang behind. In El Salvador tattoos are enough to have you barred from schools and sometimes even medical treatment. They can also be a signal to police or freelance vigilantes that result in harassment, violence and even death. In Guatemala it is not uncommon for vigilante death squads to use tattoos to mark the young for extermination. Tattoos are difficult to get rid of in a safe (and inexpensive) fashion. In El Salvador, for example, it is reported that there is only one tattoo-removing machine for the whole country.

Honduras, Guatemala, Nicaragua, El Salvador, Jamaica, South Africa, Nigeria, Kenya) gang gear may be scarce or simply too expensive. In urban Central America or Port Moresby and Lea in Papua New Guinea, gangs tend to use body identifiers such as tattoos and scarring rather than the latest athletic gear. Tattoos are also a prominent feature of the Mara gangs that dominate south of the Mexican border.

The rituals of the gang pseudo-family include initiation, loyalty tests, a knowledge and pride in gang history and exploits, and a strong sense of "us" versus "them." Other gang indicators are the use of a series of hand signs and the ubiquitous "tagging" graffiti (from the Italian

Gang Games

These days anyone can be a gangster – with no risk of getting shot. The video gaming industry produces a plethora of interactive computer games. Games such as the controversial *Grand Theft Auto: San Andreas*, *Halo 2* and *25 to Life* allow you to gun down as much of the opposition as you like. In *25 to Life* you can be a gangster or a cop and use a variety of weapons to get your way. *Bulletproof* (Universal Vivendi Games) contains a biography of rapper 50 Cent, who uses an arsenal of weapons to navigate his way through the underworld.

The US Army has entered the violent video game market with the $6.3 million-dollar *America's Army*, a kind of recruiting device. The Internet game has 60,000 visitors daily firing over 2 million rounds of ammunition. It has been downloaded 30 million times and 20 to 40 percent of new army recruits have played the game.

Most of these games are bought by consumers who are living out a fantasy. But as researcher Craig Anderson puts it, "all the studies show the same thing and that is [that] exposure to violent video games is associated with increases in aggressive behavior."[5] Anderson points out that unlike in films and TV the game participant is actually involved in the decision to shoot and kill. Further, the glorification of gang lifestyles increases the cultural tolerance for violence in a way that does not reflect the real dangers and hardships faced by both gang members and their communities. But 50 Cent has no doubts: "the video game definitely captures the essence of who I am."[6]

word for scratching) that announces a gang presence in urban areas. These are cheap ways for a gang to give its members a visible sense of belonging. If you combine tattooing with tags and hand signals, it becomes quite an art to translate the meanings of the different gang cultures. Brazil is a center of some of the most creative contemporary graffiti.

As gangs become more sophisticated and sink their roots deeper into the underground economy, at least the upper layers of gang leadership tend to forego signifiers that make them identifiable to the police or to opposing gangs. Gang veterans buy suits and have their tattoos scrubbed as their stake in criminal enterprises becomes more lucrative.

Gangsta Rap

Street gang culture is caught up in the wider hip hop culture of which graffiti is also a part. This is a complicated relationship. Much of hip hop culture — the graffiti, the music, the dancing, the drug scene, the computer games, the body art — has nothing to do with gangs. However a part of hip hop culture has been taken over by gang culture.

The big record labels have consistently promoted a subset of hip hop called "gangsta rap," which glorifies guns and the gang lifestyle, cashing in on the gritty realism of the street. Some big names in hip hop are associated with this trend — Ice-T, 50 Cent, the Notorious B.I.G. (Biggie Smalls), Scarface and the white rapper from Detroit, Eminem.

While gangsta rap has many roots, most in the know trace the definitive breakthrough to the N.W.A. (aka Niggaz With Attitude) album *Straight Outta Compton* in 1988. The group and the West Coast recording firm Ruthless Records grew out of the LA crack scene. The main man behind both was a former Compton drug dealer named Eazy-E. Their controversial track "Fuck tha Police" set the tone for an explosion of gritty gangsta rap productions glorifying gang identities.

This was by no means just a sales technique — within six months of each other two feuding gangsta superstars Tupac Shakur (Death Row Records) and Biggie Smalls (Bad Boy Entertainment) were gunned down. Tupac took five slugs outside Quad Studios in New York in November 1994 and was fatally shot in September 1996. Biggie met his demise after leaving a music industry party in LA the following March. 50 Cent and Big L were also wounded by gunshot. 50 Cent continues as a one-man industry, his name connected with everything from gangsta films to video games. But not all rappers have been so lucky. More than sixty rappers in the US have been murdered in the last two decades.

Music journalists Rodrigo Bascuñán and Christian Pearce in *Enter the Babylon System* trace what they see as a degeneration of hip hop from a vital form expressing the grit and pain of the ghetto to a corrupted exposition of gratuitous violence.[7] They point to hip hop "product placement" of handguns, such as the Glock and the Desert Eagle, and automatic weapons, like the Uzi and the MAC-9. The journalists identify seventeen songs that mention Glocks in their titles alone.

But the trend of violent glitz and crude "Get Rich or Die Tryin'" (50 Cent) materialism does not go unchallenged. Many rappers are appalled by the sellout of the motto "Keep it Real" to romanticized violence.

In 1989 KRS-One and Chris D from Public Enemy helped organize the single "Self-Destruction" to address the violence in the music and the community. It is a thin line between rap that expresses the pain and violence of poverty, and rap that glorifies violence to sell itself. But it is the judgment of even enthusiasts like Bascuñán and Pearce that the pendulum has swung dramatically to the latter.

Rap's relationship to gangs has moved beyond the borders of the US and there are variations (often fused with other musical traditions) in most other parts of the world.[8] Other musical forms are also part of gang identity, depending on the place and tradition. In the Caribbean, reggae still rules as the music dealing with life on the mean streets of Trenchtown (Kingston, Jamaica) or Port-of-Spain (Trinidad). Again, there is a tension between songs that glorify gangs and a more sophisticated reggae associated with Bob Marley and others that gives a nuanced and bittersweet sense of life on the street. Gangsters (mostly battle-hardened adult criminals) who work in the huge narco-trafficker gangs currently terrorizing Mexico are often glorified in *narcocorridos* — danceable pop songs that spread the appeal for Mexico's most wanted among impressionable youth.

In Brazil the main gang music is Proibidão (forbidden), a kind of funk with rap influences. The music is localized to particular favelas since its message promoting gangs and crime is illegal for play on Brazilian airwaves. The gangs hold *bailes* (dances) where the music is played and DJs shout out the message of loyalty to their particular gang and hatred for opposition gangs and the authorities. These illegal *bailes* are used to recruit the young into gangs. Proibidão is particularly identified with Comando Vermelho. While official society regards Proibidão as just the promoter of violence-laden gang messages, its practitioners regard it as a legitimate expression of the hardship of favela experience — a debate that echoes the disputes in North American hip hop and gangsta rap.

But it's not just the poets of nihilism and the record companies that promote them that are to blame. There is no shortage of violence within the larger entertainment industry. Hollywood has been churning it out at least since *Scarface* and other gangster movies of the 1930s. Everything from the fashion industry to gaming and comics helps shape a "bad boy" style that too many try to live up to.

Guns Rule

The gun has become the main identifier of gang life. Songs, games and films may promote gang appeal but it is the fetish for the weapon itself that is the centerpiece of gang identity. There is no shortage of small arms (i.e., portable weapons) in the world. There are an estimated

639 million (roughly one for every ten people) with 60 percent of them in civilian hands. On average, 500,000 people a year are killed with small arms.[9]

The manufacture of guns and the manufacture of gang identities go hand in hand. The small arms industry is big business, the prerogative of a relatively few countries, the most prominent of which is the US. The guns in the songs and on the streets come primarily from places like the Magnum factory in Minneapolis (the Desert Eagle) or Smyrna, Georgia (where they put together the Glock). If it's a high-tech automatic weapon like the Tec-9, it's probably from Miami, a MAC-10 is from the Military Armament Corporation in Georgia, and a MAC-11 is from the Cobray Company in North Dakota. There are many other gun manufacturers around the world, like the Kalashnikov (AK series) from Russia or the Uzi from Israel. The French and the British both have big industries. Their weapons end up in some of the poorest parts of Africa and Asia. But if you live in the Americas, chances are the gun you own or that ends up threatening you is of US manufacture.

It has long been a complaint of countries caught up in the drug war that US-made guns provide the protection that allows the drug trade to flourish. The US puts pressure on countries like Jamaica, Colombia, Bolivia and Mexico to stop the flow of drugs. In the meantime the street gangs that are the foot soldiers of the drug trade are arming themselves with weapons smuggled in from the US. Jamaican authorities have consistently traced illegal firearms and crime guns back to their source in the factories of the United States.[10] In Mexico, with much stricter gun laws than the United States, the *Miami Herald* reports that 95 percent of confiscated guns were bought legally in the US.

In the meantime, a ferocious gun lobby in the US ensures that there is little government restriction of gun ownership and manufacture. The centerpiece of the gun lobby is the National Rifle Association (NRA), which maintains that the right to bear arms is of equal weight to the right to free speech and the right to vote. Woe betide the politician who tries to stand up to the NRA. Even such an obvious liberal as President Barack Obama ducks the gun issue. The NRA's blacklist of anti-gun "baddies" include the American Medical Association and the National Association of School Psychologists. The NRA and the plethora of gun publications like *Guns and Ammo* and *Shooting Times* are lavishly underwritten through ads and grants from the small arms industry. Together they help maintain a gun-tolerant violent society in the US that has the highest homicide and crime rates in the Global North. It is a violence that spills over US borders along with the export of weaponry.

The late former actor Charlton Heston, as president of the NRA, reached the heights of hypocrisy with his campaign against violent rap music, especially Ice-T's *Body Count*.[11] It is a common practice of advocates of "the right to bear arms" to divert attention away from gun culture and onto the violent parts of popular music, computer games and films. They make a handy scape-goat. In fact it is the gun that is the root, not the branch. So it is the conservative partisans of lax gun laws who are the natural allies of violent gangsters, not the liberal advocates of a sensible criminology that moves beyond heavy-handed police tactics.

Gang appeal is a combination of broader (profitable) cultural currents that interact with conditions of poverty and hopelessness to create an attractive pseudo-empow-erment that the "gang family" provides. Tack onto this the economic opportunities offered by the underground drug economy, and you have a potent mix that has fueled the explosive growth of street gangs since the early 1980s. This mix doesn't appear about to change any time soon.

Chapter 6
The Politics of Gangs

> The people accept gangsters as the lesser of two
> evils, as the state that cannot protect its citizens
> or manifest any visible signal of its own legitimate
> right to rule will not command any allegiance.
> — Adam Elkus[1]

The explosion of young street gangs globally can be traced
back to the 1980s. It was in this period that a whole
series of gang-related and youth violence issues came to
the fore — the crack cocaine epidemic, the child soldier,
the narco-trafficker, the epidemic of gun violence, rising
crime rates. The causes were myriad. Exploding urban
populations. The escalation of civil conflict. The growth
of radical inequality associated with the "pamper the
rich" policies of Ronald Reagan and Margaret Thatcher
that spread throughout the world thanks to the policies of the World Bank and the International Monetary
Fund. This triggered a retreat of both state and market
from the rapidly growing poor communities in both the
North and the South. This is the situation that we are

still living with today. The abandoned poor are left to make their own way in a downright hostile world. The result is a chaotic situation of "might makes right" in which contemporary gang logic thrives. Hawkish Western governments entered into the logic of Cold War escalation by backing often autocratic proxy governments throughout the Global South. The only criteria were anti-Communist credentials.

The Retreat from Justice

There were other possibilities at the time. Central America, in particular, saw an insurgency rise up against some of the most despotic and ruthless dictatorships in the world. In Nicaragua the Sandinista movement came to power with a social justice agenda that set off alarm bells in the Reagan White House. Elsewhere in the region similar challenges were being mounted. Liberation movement challenges to the military regimes in Guatemala and El Salvador brought unwelcome fantasies of another Cuba or two in the Western Hemisphere.

The youth of Central America, in particular, rallied to the cause of social transformation, at no small risk to life and limb. The US response was to ramp up support for their allies in the region, flooding it with guns that found their way into the hands of the security forces of the dictatorships and the Contra guerilla movement sponsored by the US in Honduras to attack socialist Nicaragua. The violence mounted, with hundreds killed in the Nicaragua War and in neighboring El Salvador. In Guatemala a little-known racist genocide of mostly native people was carried out by the dictatorship of the fundamentalist Christian General Ríos Montt. Whole villages were wiped out in the brave (but in the end futile) struggle for social justice by Guatemala's indigenous majority. An estimated 200,000 people (mostly indigenous and mostly civilians) were killed.[2] The politics of impunity (few of those responsible for the genocide were ever brought to justice) helped feed the gang mentality that haunts much of Central America to this day. It is not economic benefit that has "trickled down," as believers in the unrestrained free market would have it — what has trickled down is the idea that ruthlessness and criminality can escape punishment.

The political fallout was obvious. By the 1990s the Sandinistas had been banished and the status quo had triumphed in the rest of Central America. Idealism and the young's hopes for change receded and hopelessness and despair re-took the stage. The region was flooded with guns and young people who had experience of armed conflict but little hope of employment. There was also a dramatic increase in the entrepreneurial opportunities connected with the drug trade. The US had managed to curtail trafficking routes through the Caribbean, and there was an increase in demand for South American cocaine due to the development of the relatively inexpensive crack cocaine movement (known on the street as "rock"). The new routes were through Central America to Mexico.

US authorities added to the problem by expelling thousands of Central American-born juveniles (many directly after they were released from prison) who had learned their gang trade on the streets of East Los Angeles. It is here that the two Salvadoran-based gangs Mara Salvatrucha and Calle 18 (known collectively as Maras) have their roots. These young gangsters landed back in their countries of birth (predominantly El Salvador but also Honduras and Guatemala) with few economic prospects and lots of gang experience. The result of all this was a "perfect storm" for the growth of youth violence and gang culture.

In Nicaragua youth gangs (known as *pandillas*) are also a big problem but they are more local and less violent than their counterparts elsewhere.[3] Part of the reason for this is that there was less of a connection between Nicaragua and the gang heartland of Los Angeles. Nicaraguan emigration to the US went primarily to Florida and was made up of a more prosperous group (self-exiled from the Sandinistas) than those seeking to escape the poverty and brutality of the neighboring military dictatorships.

The judgment of one study of gang activities in Central America cuts to the core of the problem: "Gangs have become convenient scapegoats on which to blame the isthmus's problems and through which those in power attempt to maintain an unequal status quo."[4]

A similar process of suppressed social justice can be seen in the black ghettos of major US cities. After the assassination of civil rights leader Martin Luther King in Memphis on April 4, 1968, the philosophy of non-violence lost momentum and some angry black activists shifted to the idea of self-defense against the white police force and power structure. In the late 1960s and into the 1970s the Black Panther Party (formed in 1966), gained more adherents to its black liberation cause, using both legal and illegal methods. The police came down hard on the Panthers, using informants, infiltrators and police raids. Many of the party's leaders, including Huey Newton and Fred Hampton, were assassinated. Some Panthers contributed to the decline of the BPP by themselves glorifying violence. On the other hand, the Panthers ran school breakfast programs and community health clinics. The FBI worked to increase the animosity between the BPP and street gangs such as Chicago's Blackstone Rangers. Although the BPP were at times engaged in semi-criminal activity, in general they seemed to be working for the greater community.

With the demise of the BPP in the late 1970s, the organizational vacuum left behind in the black ghettos of cities like Chicago and Los Angeles was largely filled by violent young street gangs. These gangs had little of the BPP's commitment to the community and the larger social justice struggle. They quickly got involved in the drug trade and various extortion rackets. In a way they reflected the everyone-for-themselves spirit of the materialistic 1980s. In both the ghettos of US cities and the poverty-ridden slums of Central America, the explosion of gang violence is a byproduct of the failure of more rational kinds of protest.

In Brazil too the start of the street gangs of Rio and São Paulo dates from the overthrow of the reformist Goulart government in the 1960s. The nucleus of gangs like Rio's Red Command were defeated revolutionaries who had opposed the country's military dictatorship.[5]

Post-liberation Blues

Street gang violence grows not only after the repression of social justice movements but when those movements succeed but fail to deliver the goods. The political trigger factor varies, but the consequence is the same—a vacuum created by a decline in political idealism.

In South Africa the course followed by the African National Congress of ensuring financial stability by protecting the interests of investors and the better-off members of society (both black and white) has left the country's poor majority with dashed hopes. It was these poor people who had formed the backbone of the resistance that allowed the ANC to overthrow the country's apartheid system. The youth gangs that dominate many of South Africa's black townships had sometimes played a dubious role in this struggle, sometimes colluding with the police of the apartheid state to target ANC activists. But most of South Africa's black youth identified with the struggle and many were active in it. So the frustration of expectations for a better life and an alleviation of poverty under the ANC is a bitter pill to swallow. Here is how the head of South Africa's Centre for the Study of Violence and Reconciliation Amanda Dissel sees it:

Frustration, resulting from the non-delivery of material benefits by the government, has led many youth and adults to seek opportunities to acquire wealth elsewhere. Crime is an obvious alternative.[6]

Dissel was speaking in the late 1990s but youth crime in South Africa continues to be a major problem. For the white (and increasingly black) elite, life is lived in gated communities guarded by private security firms. Although no one is completely safe it is the poor, mostly black or "colored" communities that suffer most from youth gang violence. Like Central America the post-conflict situation is one that left many weapons unaccounted for. It's a simple formula: weapons + poverty + inequality + dashed hopes = street gang violence.

Another example of gang violence moving into the vacuum created by frustrated hope is in East Timor in the South Pacific. Following a successful liberation struggle against Indonesia, East Timor proclaimed its independence in 2002. Timorese gang groups known as the Petitioners caused a major stir in February 2008 when they attacked and seriously wounded President José Ramos-Horta.

These gangs are deeply rooted and were frequently involved in defending their communities during the early 1970s when the country was occupied by Indonesia. In their origins they are quite diverse, ranging from disaffected veterans, members of village youth groups and martial arts organizations. Their growth has taken place due to economic grievances and the weakness of public and security institutions in the country.

According to the Small Arms Survey (an independent Geneva-based research group), there is an overlap in gang membership with the security forces and some political groups. Conflict between gangs often follows inter-communal and other ethnic tensions. Today the streets and buildings of Dili, the capital, are marked with gang "tags" that in many ways resemble the streets of black South Central or Latino East Los Angeles. So far, however, the gangs do not have access to the sophisticated weaponry that characterizes gangs elsewhere.[7] The liberation from Communism after the fall of the Berlin Wall in 1989 also led to disappointment with the unified Germany's newly minted capitalism. One of the results was the growth of racist skinhead gangs in the former East Germany and Russia (see White Racist Gangs, page 65).

The Criminalized State

The growth of criminal gangs often occurs in situations where government is corrupt. Criminal networks in many places have infiltrated a state institution or even the state as a whole. In Mexico it is now widely accepted that narco-traffickers have broad influence inside the police, judiciary and other branches of government. In Central America and Brazil there is ample evidence of this. The police are particularly subject to corruption although they are by no means alone. In Guatemala, in February 2007, three Salvadoran politicians were murdered, apparently by members of a police unit charged with fighting organized crime — and then the four suspected killers were themselves silenced by bullets in police jail cells. It is unlikely that this could have been done without further police collusion. In gang-ridden Rio former police chief Álvaro Lins and a former state governor are up on charges of corruption.[8] The police are often poorly paid and little regulated and so seek opportunities outside their official role, either by working with gangs (to get access to drug profits) or hiring themselves out as death squads to get rid of troublesome street youth and beggars.

This development of the criminalized state is in the most severe cases known as the "failed state." There are many examples of this in recent history — the West African states of Liberia and Sierra Leone, the warlord-ridden East African territory of Somalia and the desperately poor Caribbean island nation of Haiti, to name a few. In such cases the society is rent apart by armed criminal factions led by warlords or gangs organized around tribal, religious or local community affiliation.

Child soldiers are often a symptom of these failed states. While not part of the kind of urban street gangs that haunt the poor neighborhoods of many major cities, the child soldier shares many of the characteristics of gang members. They are often "recruited" from village youth, frequently simply through kidnapping. While most street gangs have at least some elements of self-governance, the child soldier is mostly governed directly by adult warlords or criminal networks that use them as cannon fodder in their criminal/political enterprise. Charles Taylor, former president of Liberia, is perhaps the most notorious of this kind of warlord politician. Taylor is on trial by the United Nations International Criminal Court in the Hague for crimes against humanity. He ruled Liberia as a kind of criminalized terror state between August 1997 and August 2003. He used child soldiers as part of his militia in Liberia, but also when he launched a bloody civil war in neighboring Sierra Leone in order to control that country's lucrative diamond trade.

Taylor is not alone. There are many others like him who may be associated with the constant shifting struggle for power in places like Somalia and the Congo. The Lord's Resistance Army, a rebel group in Northern Uganda, is particularly notorious for dragooning village youth into their war against the government in Kampala —boys as soldiers and girls as prostitutes. Young children are often forced to engage in the killing of their own families as a kind of rite of passage.

The stories of several child soldiers are now on record (as published memoirs or testimonies given to international organizations) and they make for some pretty harrowing reading. They are often recruited against their will, and the initiation to which they are subjected makes the street gang version (committing some crime or act of violence) pretty tame. Once this rupture with normality has been imposed on a vulnerable psyche, loyalty can be demanded and a sense of identity re-established. This is an extreme version of what happens when adolescent youth join street gangs.

Another parallel is the use of drugs to keep the recruit off balance and subject to whatever demands their superiors might make of them. The cult of the gun and the power it commands (to someone who has had precious little power) is also an intoxicating part of the mix. The militias that these child soldiers are forced to join are notoriously unstable, and when they break up or are defeated it is very difficult for disoriented young recruits to regain any sense of normality. Programs aimed at reintegrating former gang members in Liberia and Sierra Leone in West Africa have found the process notoriously tricky. Yet without the help of sensitive programs of reorientation they may just drift back into a life of gangsterism.

It is important to keep in mind that such youth gangs (particularly in areas of power vacuum and corruption) are subject to manipulation by adult political forces. While it is the gang that catches the headlines for its criminal outrages, it is often the power-hungry politician behind the scenes who is the puppeteer.

Haiti is a notorious case in point. Gangs in the slums of Port-au-Prince's Cité Soleil have played a big political role on the island. Cité Soleil has 300,000 residents and 90 percent of the children are too poor to go to school.

An alliance of disaffected gangsters and opposition politicians launched the assault that resulted in the overthrow of populist President Aristide in 2004. And

Aristide had his own gang allies. Slum gangs fought pitched battles with the UN peacekeeping forces in Port-au-Prince with passive support from their communities, who tended to see the UN troops as occupiers complicit in getting rid of Aristide, who remained the champion of the poor.

The hopes once associated with Aristide left a vacuum that only gangs could fill. The capture of the notorious gang leader Evens (in his mid-twenties) and several others in 2007 has somewhat reduced the tension. Today the slums of Haiti still have a significant gang presence that carries out kidnapping of wealthy Haitians and the occasional foreigner. In another blowback situation Haitian gangs have started to become active in Florida. Prospere Borgelin, who works with the International Committee of the Red Cross (ICRC), points out that while things have improved, "Misery breeds violence and there is still plenty of misery in Cité Soleil."[9] Following the earthquake that devastated Port-au-Prince in early 2010, the fragile progress against gangs was undermined as hundreds of dangerous gang members escaped prison. Gangs started to prey on insecure quake victims and kidnap NGO personnel sent to help in the relief effort.

In neighboring Jamaica the posses have been traditionally associated with one of the two main political parties — the Labor Party and the National Party. During election campaigns the posses of each side would violently disrupt the rallies and campaign activities of the opposing party. This reached its heyday in the 1970s and 1980s, a turbulent period in Jamaican politics. These days gang activity in Kingston has lost much of its political character and has fallen back into being a straight criminal enterprise.

The history of youth gangs and politics remains a complex one and difficult to unpick. In the nineteenth century US street gangs formed the basis of urban political machines that, mostly through the Democratic Party, formed the vehicle for ethnic communities (the Irish and the Italians) to gain political power. Corruption and patronage have always been part of the process — it is not what you know but who you know. The police and other forces of order remain tainted by their gang contacts, particularly when lucrative pay-offs from the drug trade may be on offer.

In contemporary times, with high-tech weapons added into the mix in a world marred by the extremes of economic inequality and political instability, the stakes have become even higher. It should surprise no one that in a culture where the powerful regularly commit crimes ranging from mass fraud to murder that youth gangs learn from the example set by their elders. In a culture of impunity where those with power are only infrequently identified as the authors of such crimes, "gangthink" should be seen as a logical (if perverted) assertion of — "they're stealing up there at the top, so we are going to steal too."

Chapter 7
The Assault on Youth

> When "zero tolerance" replaced "teaching toler-
> ance" as the dominant paradigm for children's
> lives and public education, society unleashed noth-
> ing less than a low-grade, persistent war on youth
> — and on our common future.
> — Bernardine Dohrn[1]

The rise of youth gangs needs to be seen against the backdrop of the issue of youth in general. As French historian
and medievalist Philippe Ariès has shown, childhood (as
we know it in the North) did not exist until the seven-
teenth century. Until this time, children were treated as
little adults expected to contribute (through their labor)
and take responsibility just like other adults. Most children in the poor Global South have never escaped this
status. Even in the Global North informal and formal
child labor has always been the lot of the marginalized
and the excluded. Some of the children of wealth, on
the other hand, never grow up at all, living a life of
consumer-drugged perpetual adolescence.

The advance of compulsory education has made some inroads into "little adult" status almost everywhere. With education began the romanticization of childhood as a glorious period of innocence and discovery. Now children's special status puts them in a category deserving protection and special treatment. Public policy aims to alleviate "child poverty" as if it could somehow be separated from the supposedly more deserved adult version.

There is a moral panic about children and their sexuality yet at the same time children are continuously sexualized by consumer culture. NGO ads feature the begging eyes of unpromising young lives from Ethiopia to Cambodia: "Can't you help? Please adopt this foster child." In Christian countries we are exhorted in various Santa drives to ensure that even poor children can enjoy the cornucopia under the tree on Christmas morning. All this occurs against the backdrop of an arsenal of public policy measures that have undercut the social welfare state so as to give the well-to-do ever greater tax breaks.

It adds up to treating the child as "other." But with it goes the expectation that children will act in certain ways — be diligent, grateful, respectful and loving. When they don't, we get mad. That this "tender trap," constructed of various hypocrisies, is mostly a myth is something kids themselves see through very quickly. When faced with an unpromising future, children are less likely than adults to shrug philosophically and mutter, "oh well." Youth revolt in such circumstances can take on many forms.

Students have been the flashpoint of revolutions, as

we can see historically in places like France in 1968 and today in the streets of Tehran and Cairo. But often the revolt of the young is less coherent, shaped by the pathologies of violence and acquisitiveness of the surrounding adult world. Youth look at adult corruption and say, "So that is how the game is played." Enter the world of the street gang, the corner drug dealer, the young prostitute, the swarming, the mindless violence of peer groups, the casual brutality of the slum.

The reaction of those with power and privilege to defend is predictable — a zero-tolerance clampdown. Delinquent youth has turned itself into an easy target, a scapegoat in an unjust world. Of course this generational reaction is mixed with other factors, such as racism against criminal youth from minority cultures (native gangs in the Canadian West, Australia and New Zealand, blacks and Hispanics in the US, Muslims in Europe, Chechen gangs in Russia, South Asian gangs in the UK), a fear of the "uncontrollable" poor (in the mega-slums of Africa and Latin America), and the love of order so dear to the hearts of conservatives everywhere. This has proved a powerful political card for the Right to play on the legitimate fears of violent crime. In the North there is increasing pressure to get rid of the juvenile justice system and have the young offender be treated as an adult so they can be sentenced to some hard time. In the Global South, where mass incarceration is just too expensive, responses vacillate between total neglect of poor communities and arbitrary vigilante-style street justice.

The arsenal of repression in the fight against youth crime is truly impressive. Here are some of the highlights.

The No-Go Area

Large areas of major cities such as Rio and São Paulo in Brazil, Port-au-Prince in Haiti, Nairobi in Kenya and Cape Town in South Africa have been more-or-less abandoned to gang rule. These are areas where the authorities have virtually given up trying to improve the lives of citizens. In the vast Makoko slum of Lagos, in Nigeria, the Area Boys are a law unto themselves with police a rare and not particularly welcome presence.[2]

The no-go area strategy adopted by the authorities aims to isolate lawless slums, abdicating all government responsibility. If the police do enter it is usually as a violent invading force. The murders, extortion and crime that haunt such places are seen to be a tragic but inevitable consequence of mass poverty. They seldom make the news unless some more privileged sector of society is affected. No-go areas also exist, to a lesser but still significant degree, in the black slums of US cities like Chicago and LA.[3]

The Police Sweep

Police assault a gang-ridden area in waves, "sweeping up" a large number of suspects, many of whom typically have little to do with gang activities. This is a tactic also used by the US forces against the urban insurgency in places like Iraq. It gives police a lot of visibility and credit for "doing something," especially when seizures and arrests are presented at the next day's press conference.

Police are widely criticized for being indiscriminate (based on little intelligence about who the key gang leaders are) and alienating communities. Most of those arrested in such sweeps are either never charged or never convicted.

A gang worker in Toronto described a sweep he had witnessed where officers were doing "high fives" after handcuffing a mother in front of her small children. His response: "You can imagine how these kids now feel about the law."[4]

Tough Sentencing

The movement to "get tough" on youth crime promotes mandatory minimum sentences (undercutting judicial discretion), pushing youth into the adult criminal justice system and special gang-related provisions to increase sentencing. It originated in the US but has spread to nearly every other country. In the US in 2005 Congress passed the Gang Deterrence and Community Protection Act, which defined non-violent drug trafficking as a violent crime, resulting in draconian sentences. Canada has followed suit with crime bill C-15, which provides mandatory minimum sentences for a number of gang-related crimes. One of the more severe sentencing provisions was California's Proposition 6 (the so-called Safe Neighborhoods Act) that would have thrown juveniles into adult court (subjecting them to more severe sentences) if "gang-related" was added to a charge, even if the accused weren't gang members.[5] It was defeated in a 2008 ballot but there are similar efforts in the pipeline both inside and outside US borders.

Social Cleansing

In countries where widespread incarceration is beyond the capacity of the state, the social cleansing solution is an alternative strategy for the war on youth. In some of the mega-cities of Latin America, and to a lesser extent

- Sweeping policies don't allow for judgment on a case-by-case basis.
- Educators are turned into auxiliaries of the police, or the police themselves are used inside educational institutions, creating an atmosphere not conducive to learning.
- Severe rules often catch fairly petty infringements. For example, here are some of the "crimes" caught in the zero tolerance net in US schools: A Utah boy was suspended for giving his cousin a cold pill prescribed to both students; in Rhode Island a kindergartner was suspended for bringing a plastic knife to school so he could cut cookies; fifth-graders in California who adorned their mortarboards with tiny plastic soldiers to support troops in Iraq were forced to cut off their miniature weapons.
- ZT policies are often at odds with other laws, community norms or cultural messages. For example, in the US the right to bear arms is encouraged but if you are found with them in school you can be expelled. Mixed messages abound.[6]

Africa, groups of citizens (often off-duty police) form themselves into unofficial paramilitary groups. They are frequently paid by merchants or other notables for doing their deadly work. They pick out a range of victims — gay people, prostitutes, visible minorities, the homeless, drug addicts, the mentally disturbed — although street youth, who may be part of these other target groups, are their most consistent victims.

Punishment ranges from removal from an area through beating and torture all the way to execution, sometimes on a large scale. This avoids the costly and uncertain legal processes and is perhaps the most vicious form of generational hate. It also has the effect of strengthening the allegiance of poor youth to street gangs as a question of survival.

Guatemala, Colombia and Brazil saw the first examples of this vigilante action in the late 1980s and remain the murderous centers of this particular form of war against the young (and others). In Brazil, for example, an estimated 7 million homeless children are often forced to survive through petty criminal acts and are subject to "elimination" by members of the police, both on and off duty.[7]

Human Rights Watch reports that police in São Paulo and Rio de Janeiro were involved in 11,000 extrajudicial "resistance killings" (where the accused supposedly resisted police in some way) between 2003 and 2009.[8]

Non-criminal Sanctions

When criminal charges aren't enough a range of other sanctions can be employed to deal with wayward youth. Curfews, anti-social behavior orders (ASBOs), the total surveillance environment with closed circuit TV cameras and extensive computer networking by authorities, and behavior modification drugs are all used to control youth movement and activity.

At least 500 US cities have curfews on teenage youth, including 78 of the 92 cities with a population over 180,000. In most of these cities, curfews prohibit children under 18 from being on the streets after 11:00 pm during the week and after midnight on weekends. About 100 cities also have daytime curfews to keep children off the streets during school hours. The curfews are designed to prevent crime, increase parental responsibility for their children, and give police greater ability to stop people involved in suspicious activity.

In the UK the Anti-Social Behaviour Act of 2003 created zones where police could hold and escort home youth under sixteen whether they were misbehaving or not.[9] The government of Tony Blair is responsible for the peak in youth detention in 2002 after he passed his Street Crime Initiative. The Blair government also made wide use of controversial ASBOs, which allow authorities to restrict (often young) individuals when their behavior "causes or is likely to cause harassment, alarm, or distress to one or more people who are not in the same household of the perpetrator." This covers a lot of territory. For example:

- Jack Lambeth, aged fifteen, was banned from leaving his house between 9:30 pm and 7 am for two years because of "sustained anti-social behavior" (February 2009).
- Stephen Blowes, aged fifteen, was given an order for persistently jumping over neighbors' hedges and fences (May 2008).
- Patrick and Louis Cairney, two brothers, aged nine and five, were threatened with an order

for disturbing their neighbors by "playing outside their house." (The minimum age at which a child can be given an ASBO is ten.)

Between the launching of the ASBO system in 2003 and the end of December 2007, 14,972 ASBOs were issued. By May 2008 this number had shot up 67 percent. Just under 50 percent of all ASBOs are breached, and you can receive up to five years in prison for breaching an ASBO. In other words, the system results in criminalizing non-criminal behavior.[10] It is perhaps the purest expression of shaping jurisprudence to control "disruptive" youth by their disapproving elders.

Incarceration

Many young people end up in prison. Sometimes it is a juvenile justice facility, but often it is a prison where most of the other inmates are hard-core criminals. In most prisons in the Americas and in parts of Africa gangs predominate. To survive in prisons it is often necessary to seek the protection of such gangs. The gangs may reflect street gangs outside prison, or they may be organized around racial divisions (most US maximum and medium security prisons are dominated by black, Hispanic and white gangs). Without gang protection, in many places prisoners are subject to violence, rape, exploitation and even death. Learning gang ways and criminal techniques, developing contacts and affiliations easily turns the impressionable young offender into a hardened gang member.

Brazil is a good example of how overcrowded and dismal prison conditions can provoke gang violence. In May 2006 the São Paulo street gang Primeiro Comando da Capital (First Capital Command, PCC) launched a prison revolt in 100 prisons across the state. The revolt was coordinated with attacks on police stations and vehicles by PCC members using bombs and automatic weapons. The police struck back, killing 122 "suspected criminals" (28 of whom turned out to have no criminal record). São Paulo, a city of 19 million people, was brought to a terrified halt.

You need go no further than the US — a country with 5 percent of the world's population and 25 percent of the world's prisoners — to understand the failure of the mass incarceration of youth. The imprisonment of huge numbers of youth (mostly for relatively minor crimes) ensures a new generation of gang members cycling back into the streets.

In the US it is estimated that just 3 percent of inmates held in federal and state institutions are gang members (this amounts to tens of thousands), but they are responsible for over 50 percent of the problems in the prison system. This may be a severe underestimation. According to Michael Chettleburgh in his book on Canadian gangs, at least 50 percent of prisoners in medium and maximum security prisons are gang-affiliated. If this is true one could expect US figures to be much higher. Chettleburgh refers to prison as Crime School or Gladiator School, where young gangsters learn their trade.[11] As in Brazil, even when they're imprisoned, gang members continue to control much of the crime on the street — ordering hits, making deals, dividing up territory and raking in profits.

Youth incarceration is an issue in Europe as well. In France seven new penitentiary establishments for minors (EPMs) have been set up and are plagued with violence, riots and suicides. But some European countries are worse than others. In the UK there are 3000 children in detention facilities while in other European countries of similar population size there are many fewer. For example, France has 530 and Italy 450 children in detention. In Sweden, with 20 percent of the population of the UK, there are just six.[12]

Overcrowded prison systems pay less and less attention to rehabilitation, devoting most of their time to staying on top of a population of angry, violent inmates crammed into inadequate facilities. Studies carried out by the Atlanta-based Center for Disease Control found that youth forced into the adult criminal justice system in order to give them longer sentences report a higher level of reoffending. "Not only does it not deter youth crime, it actually makes them more violent," says Robert L. Johnson, dean of the New Jersey Medical School and a member of the CDC task force.[13]

Doing What Everybody Else Does
If you confront young gang leaders about the pernicious and violent nature of their activities, a common response

is "we are just doing what everyone else does." Before dismissing such a response it is worth weighing up the kind of examples the adult world of power provides for its children. Corruption and the use of violence to get your own way did not start, after all, with the post-1985 gang generation. Whether it's the predatory practices of a transnational oil or chemical corporation or the bullying of the US military to get its way in the Middle East or Latin America, recent history is chock-full of examples of "might makes right" — the basic philosophy of gang logic. Young people frequently hold that the police, in particular, are a gang that is often brutal, stupid and corrupt.

Corruption (as we saw in relation to inequality in Chapter 2) helps fuel street gangsterism. Transparency International rates the level of corruption around the world. With a few exceptions (e.g., New Zealand, which has a low corruption level but a big Maori gang problem), the countries with the biggest gang problems are among the most corrupt. The US ranks eighteenth, putting it behind most European and other developed countries. South Africa, Haiti, Mexico and Brazil all provide ready examples of corrupt adult behavior for gang emulation.[14]

The French political thinker Jacques Camatte saw the gang as the essential feature of modern social organization. For him powerful organizations had a strong tendency to deteriorate into self-interested gangs. Camatte said the main difference between gangs and the political cliques that run society is that "in its external relations, the political gang tends to mask the existence of the clique, since it must seduce in order to recruit." But the organizational imperative is very similar:

> The desire to belong to a gang comes from the wish to be identified with a group that embodies a certain degree of prestige, theoretical prestige for intellectuals and organizational prestige for so-called practical men...What maintains an apparent unity in the bosom of the gang is the threat of exclusion. Those who do not respect the norms are rejected with calumny; and even if they quit, the effect is the same. This threat also serves as psychological blackmail for those who remain.[15]

Camatte's views on gang logic are quite consistent with the behavior of young street gangsters living the illusion of power and haunted by the dreaded fear of exclusion.

So street gang behavior cannot be divorced from the general spirit of the times and the kind of society it is rooted in. If police and politicians and the chief executive officers of corporations act in a self-interested and sometimes corrupt fashion, can we expect much else from the poor and impressionable young? The point was made well by American sociologist Thorstein Veblen, who famously referred to our present system of acquisitive capitalism as "the predatory phase of human development" — an argument that Albert Einstein picked up on in his famous 1949 essay about an alternative to capitalism entitled *Why Socialism?*[16] This predatory mentality is mirrored perfectly in gang behavior, the main difference being that gangs reject the rules established to abet previous predators. These rules have loaded the dice in favor of a skewed system of wealth and power where hyperghettos and squatter towns have become the norm for billions of people living on less than $2 a day.

Not all such people are of course predators. It would be more appropriate to categorize them as scavengers — think of the images of people rummaging through the garbage of mainstream society, be it in Manila's steaming Payatas dump or the people picking through the recycling on the streets of Vancouver. In a way the starting point of an effective criminal justice response to gang crime should be an attempt to sort the scavengers from the predators. Most of the young attracted to gangs are just scavenging to survive in unfavorable circumstances. Scavenging is after all a useful set of skills that could be channeled to worthwhile purpose, particularly in the coming age of ecological scarcity. Predatory activity, on the other hand, needs to be discouraged, whether by hardened gangsters or big bank executives willing to put everyone's security at risk to get their hands on multimillion-dollar bonuses.

Chapter 8
A Future with Gangs

Living free from the threat of armed violence is a basic human need. It is a precondition for human development, dignity and well-being... Conflict prevention and resolution, human rights, good governance and peace building are key steps towards reducing poverty, promoting economic growth and improving people's lives.

> — Geneva Declaration on Armed Violence and Development (2006)[1]

A criminal is a person with predatory instincts without sufficient capital to form a corporation.

> — Clarence Darrow, famous US trial lawyer[2]

The idea that gangs are temporary phenomena of deviant youth that firm criminal justice policies can bring to an end is more and more an impossible fantasy. The gangs of the early twentieth century were localized and sporadic, and while many gangs are still like this many others are not. Street gangs in Brazil and Central America (as well as black and Hispanic gangs in Chicago and Maori gangs in New Zealand) are deeply embedded in their communities and societies. They have been around for generations, have older members, are rooted in local underground economies (and sometimes legal economic activity), and like it or not, are social actors in the urban cityscape. In Europe (with the exception of parts of Russia like Kazan in Tatarstan) modern street gangs are a relatively new and often episodic phenomena.

Some gangs are serious links in the networks of global criminal enterprise. Young men are no longer just passing through serious gangs but often end up staying into their thirties — particularly where gangs are viable economic institutions. The appeal of contemporary gangs is enhanced by a "resistance identity" for youth from a racially or ethnically marginalized population. They see their life chances as slim to none and calculate that throwing their lot in with the gang enterprise is not a bad career choice.

A Predator's World

If it is unlikely gangs are going to disappear, how should societies minimize their negative impact? First a little critical self-examination would help. How can we lionize the rich and the powerful — clever soldiers, corporate cutthroats, boss-like politicians, narcissistic celebrities, selfish expressions of crude national interest — and not expect the ethos of "grab it how and when you can" to inform all social life? We need to rethink the ethos of acquisitiveness and the cult of the selfish self that has become the center of consumer capitalism and find a different ethical standard to measure what is important for human beings.

Tall order. But we could at least start by tackling the growing inequality that is tearing the social fabric almost everywhere. The societies with intractable gang problems are among the most unequal in the world. It's asking a lot to expose the poverty-stricken young to the glitz and glamor of the rich suburbs of Johannesburg, the glitter of the Champs Elysées, or the magnificent villas perched over the slums of Port-au-Prince and not have them find it all unfair. The growing global inequality that really took off in the 1980s (the point when global gang activity exploded) is not an accident. A set of policies that goes under the title of "neoliberalism" — cuts in public spending, less regulation on corporations, privatization of resources and services, more security for corporate profits, reduced taxes on the wealthy — has consciously set out to create an ever more unequal world. These policies have pushed governments everywhere away from their responsibilities to poorer citizens and let the free play of the private market decide people's economic fates. The idea is that if the private pot gets fuller all will eventually benefit. But the "trickle down" effect doesn't seem to be working. It is more like that 1950s crooner Frank Sinatra had it when he sang about "how the rich get rich and the poor get poorer."

The bloom is off the rose of neoliberalism (although

it continues to have many enthusiastic conservative supporters) as the costs continue to mount. There is a chance to start to alter the "me first" ethical standard by shaping an economic agenda that puts equality at the center of its vision. The ideas are all out there — fairer taxation, housing rights for the poor (especially squatters), support for small farmers, daycare and family support services, empowerment of women, free and relevant education and community health care, a refunding of municipal services for all communities, policing that is rooted in and for poor communities. To achieve this will of course be a gargantuan struggle.

Levels of wealth would need to be significantly reduced and endemic corruption tackled to provide a part of the necessary economic surplus. The resistance of those with resources is never timid and often brutal. It would take a steady hand to counter all the disinformation and disruption that money can buy. But setting greater equality as the major focus of public policy could significantly reduce the attractions of risky gang involvement. It would give poor people something to lose where they now have little.

End the War on Drugs
If there is one single action that could cut the ground out from under the gang economy it would be the decriminalization of drugs. The government of Mexico (perhaps the country most plagued by drug violence) has already come to this conclusion and has decriminalized the

possession of small quantities of all drugs. Mexico's aim is to undercut police corruption (drugs are frequently planted on those arrested to solicit bribes) and to shift the emphasis on enforcement to major narco-traffickers.

The War on Drugs is notable for its almost absolute failure. It has put hundreds of thousands of people (often young, black and Hispanic) into the US prison system. The US prison system is crammed with drug prisoners (50 percent of the total prisoner population). The US also spends some $40 billion every year trying to stop the trade in illegal drugs and tens of thousands of people are employed in this effort.[3] But by almost all measures this has hardly made a dint in the demand for and consumption of illegal drugs.

The effect outside the US of this drug war is even more pernicious. Whether it's the opium-producing areas of Asia or the cocaine-producing regions of the Andes, the War on Drugs has criminalized small farmers, distorted local economies, empowered gangs of ruthless traffickers and corrupted public life. Supplier countries like Colombia and Afghanistan and transit states like Guatemala and Mexico have been plunged into a virtual civil war over control of the trade and official attempts to stamp it out. Illegal status has pushed drug prices to astronomical levels, providing continuing motivation for involvement in all levels of the trade from simple farming to high-tech smuggling and money-laundering. Drug profits have not only gone to make a small group of criminals fabulously wealthy, but they have been used for bribes to pay off police and the judiciary, and to fund vigilante death squads and guerrilla insurgencies such as those of the Taliban in Afghanistan or the FARC in Colombia. The attempts at eradication (of crops) and interdiction (intercepting drugs on their way to market) — two favorite drug-war terms — have been largely funded through US aid policies. This aid could otherwise be used to tackle issues of poverty and inequality.

The decriminalization of drugs would:

- Reduce drug prices from artificially high levels, making involvement in the drug economy less attractive.
- Ensure greater quality control of drugs, making them less harmful than in conditions of illegality where they are often cut with dangerous substances.
- Provide tax revenues (from drug sales) for the public coffers that could be used to deal with the problems of at-risk youth and the health consequences of drug addiction.
- Make the drug user the main person liable for the negative consequences of use (if there are any) as opposed to the community as a whole, which now must bear the costs associated with drug-connected crime.
- Stop the expensive clogging of the criminal justice system, which negatively affects policing and courts in many countries.

Drug addiction is a public health problem and needs to be treated as such through regulation, counseling, treatment and public education. The desire of human beings to use mind-altering substances has been with us for centuries and cannot be effectively dealt with through the criminal justice system. Millions use such drugs and manage to live productive lives. It is quite arbitrary to decide that some drugs — say marijuana and hashish — are illegal and others like alcohol and tobacco are not. In conditions of illegality levels of drug use have not dropped significantly, whereas in conditions of legality (but restriction and public education) the use of nicotine has. The use of more addictive drugs (heroin, for example) could be controlled in such a fashion. Some harm from drug use is inevitable; criminalizing this use not only fails to eliminate the harm but spreads it to millions of people who are not users.

Alcohol prohibition in the US from 1920 to 1933 led to the development of a gangster economy that featured widespread corruption and drive-by shootings. This is child's play compared to the damage being done by the current War on Drugs. The procuring, transport and sale of such drugs is the oxygen that keeps many street gangs in business. It is a major source of violence as gangs fight over territorial markets and to ensure compliance in drug transactions. Entire countries are having their public life poisoned by the drug trade and the efforts to stamp it out. Without the drug trade youth gangs and violence would be significantly reduced. While not all gangs would disappear, their attraction and impact would definitely diminish.

Police Tactics

The frontline of defense against violent street gangs must of course be the police. But how this policing takes place is key to whether gangs flourish or are contained. The *mano dura* (hard hand) as practiced in Central America has long been the favorite strategy of both police and the public. The idea is to neutralize as many young gangsters as possible (through killing, imprisonment, violence and intimidation), to deplete their population and scare off new recruits. It has been a spectacular failure.

One of the consequences of this strategy is treating all gang members (hard-core leaders and wannabes) more or less the same. This high-force/low-intelligence approach reproduces simple-minded notions of good guys/bad guys that are entirely divorced from particular knowledge of gang activities and structures, inter-gang rivalries and the social conditions in which gangs are rooted. It feeds into a cycle of youth alienation from police authority, mass incarceration and high recidivism and community distrust, all of which result in the persistence of the gang problem and increased violence in the community. In many places this distrust is aggravated by police corruption and the troubling issue of poorly paid officers taking second jobs in the private security industry, where they are free to practice violence with less restraint.

Many police departments have formed gang units

known for their militaristic approach to the problem, involving sweeps, mass incarceration and crackdown on minor criminality. Tony Moreno is a famous "gang cop" from Los Angeles. After thirty-five years of experience in the Los Angeles Police Department he has become a critic of the conventional get-tough approach to dealing with gangs.

According to Moreno, the police need to become involved more broadly with the welfare of poor communities, helping with referrals to social service agencies and using a less coercive approach to youth. What makes Moreno stand out is that he knows something about gangs in general and about the specific gangsters in the LA area. This includes the crucial information about who is at the center of gang activities and who is in a peripheral orbit around a gang — vital knowledge to help wean young wannabes away from gangs. Moreno gets this knowledge by knowing and talking to gangsters in a respectful fashion — joking, asking about families, using their gang nicknames. In this way he earned his own street nickname of Pac-Man.[4]

The more intelligence-based approach is not just a question of a few maverick cops with street smarts. The gang sit-down (or call-in) is a controversial approach for law-and-order conservatives. The idea is to call major gang players into meetings to discuss issues of inter-gang tension and violence. Its most spectacular success was in Boston in 1996 where sit-downs were a key component of Operation Ceasefire, a campaign to reduce the city's youth homicide rate. Despite its sissy reputation among hard-core gang cops the call-in is a kind of focused deterrence. Sit-down organizer David Kennedy explains the approach:

Police would first identify members on parole or probation and compel them to attend a meeting. There the cops would deliver an ultimatum — the shootings must stop. And if they do not stop the consequences will be swift and certain, and severe, and punishment will be handed out not just to the individual involved in the shooting but to everyone in that individual's gang.[5]

In Boston the impact was an immediate and dramatic drop in the rate of youth homicides.

The failure of zero-tolerance policing has led to a rethink in some quarters despite a police culture that is notoriously reluctant to engage in self-critical examination. In Central America this can be seen in what is now emerging as an alternative to *mano dura* policies referred to as *mano amiga* (friendly hand) or *mano extendida* (extended hand). This approach includes reduction in violence initiatives such as voluntary weapons collection, and targeted education and public health initiatives for at-risk youth. It involves non-governmental organizations (NGOs) such as the APREDE in Guatemala, stressing approaches to reinserting gang members into the community; the JHAJA in Honduras, which offers employment opportunities to ex-gang members; and Homies Unidos, a collective of ex-gang members in El Salvador that works with gangs on alternatives to violence. But these initiatives remain on the margins of public policy.[6]

Alternatives to Gangs

Aside from moving development away from corporate profit/elite enrichment and toward equity and inclusion, a set of more specific interventions could help undercut gang power. Putting resources into community development — particularly youth programs oriented around culture and sports — would be a good start.

Viva Rio, an NGO that works on violence reduction programs in Rio de Janeiro's favelas, uses boxing clubs and tournaments to channel violent masculinity in boys between the ages of twelve and twenty-five. Girls too are now involved. Viva Rio also works as the sponsor of a sentence-diversion project in Resende just outside Rio, where it tries to keep at-risk youth out of Brazil's violent prison system. The organization has been a key player in disarmament efforts — including a voluntary small arms collection campaign, tracing the source of weapons, and trying to toughen Brazilian gun laws. It also helps coordinate a women's disarmament campaign around such slogans as "live gun-free" and "It's your gun or me" with mixed results.[7]

Viva Rio works in Haiti, where it has had some success in getting warring street gangs to abstain from violence in exchange for youth scholarships. The Haiti project, centered in the downtown Port-au-Prince community of Bel Air, is entitled Honor and Respect for Bel Air — an indication that respect and honor issues are key to unlocking the youth gang problem.[8]

The large body of experience reintegrating child soldiers, particularly in parts of Africa, could be adapted to at-risk youth who want to leave street gangs. Here too issues of self-worth are crucial.

New York City is a good example of how the problem of gangs has been tackled in a non-traditional fashion. After World War Two the city experienced an explosion of gang activity, including the classic gang rumble. High unemployment and racial segregation added fuel to the flames. In 1947 the municipal government set up the NYC Youth Board, completely autonomous from the police and criminal justice systems. Their focus was to use street gang workers to provide the critical intelligence about what was going on with young people in poor communities. They engaged in mediation efforts to resolve disputes between gangs and reduce violence. By 1965 there were 150 street workers involved in the city's most problematic neighborhoods. Some of the worst troublemakers were hired in community programs or encouraged to join the police force. The result is that although NYC is not gang-free (few major cities could claim that) gangs are small and episodic, and the city does not have the institutionalized rooted gangs that plague Los Angeles and Chicago.[9]

A commitment to understanding what is actually going on in the streets and using resources intelligently to deal with youth issues before they reach the stage of violent institutionalized gangs is key. Homeboy Industries in Los Angeles is a good example of a community project that combines the street smarts of founder Father Greg Boyle with a series of small businesses — Homeboy Bakery, Homegirl Café, Homeboy Silkscreen, Homeboy Maintenance and Homeboy Solar-Panel Installers. The recipe isn't rocket science — economic opportunity, respect, communicating in a language kids understand. The scale is small, the success modest, but real.[10]

Guns Off the Street

The gun is the icon of the gangster and if it is in short supply some of the glitter is lost from gang life, the appeal diminished. It has become an obsession with police departments almost everywhere to reduce the number of guns on the street. There are all manner of programs — seizures, turn-ins, buy-backs. Hundreds of thousands of guns have been removed and destroyed in this way.

In cities like Newark, New Jersey and Reno, Nevada, they pay for guns — no questions asked. In Caracas, the violence-ridden capital of Venezuela, over 30,000 guns were destroyed in November 2009. There is even an international day for firearms destruction — July 19.[11] The idea is that without an easy supply of weaponry gangs will become less dangerous and less violent. Yet there are still an estimated 6 million guns in Venezuela.

Guns remain in ready supply. From Glocks to Tec-9s to cheap Saturday Night Specials they have become an almost inevitable part of the underground economy. Gangs get guns in a number of ways — they are smuggled, traded in drug deals, stolen from their legal owners, obtained through the military and police, bought legally in one place and then taken to another jurisdiction where they are forbidden. Various schemes have been devised to limit the theft of guns, from safe storage laws to developing "smart guns," which would only be activated by the owner's palm print.

It is the rare gun that was not at some point legally manufactured and sold. It is here that reducing the supply of small arms could most easily take place. Gun dealers and manufacturers have an amoral approach to their business — they produce the weapons and what happens after they are sold is not their concern.

Some US cities like NYC are challenging this by suing gun dealers and manufacturers. Gun manufacturing could be produced under strict public supervision and sold only to security authorities. Even then guns and their use would have to be more tightly controlled than they are at present.

The problem is a political one. The US with its gun-mad culture and strong gun rights movement must become the target of an effective international campaign against the small arms trade. This will be difficult, as the 2008 Supreme Court decision to overturn a handgun ban that had reduced youth homicide in Washington

DC clearly shows. But it is not the US alone that needs to be targeted — Russia, Israel, China, France and many more countries profit from the small arms trade. In some countries like France and Canada, where weapons possession is strictly restricted (and gang killings far less frequent), guns are manufactured for export markets. It is hard to imagine a significant reduction in gang violence without a crackdown on the manufacture and trade in small arms.

The Future of Gangs

The Chicago School of sociologists who first examined youth gangs back in the 1920s and 1930s assumed they were transitory phenomena in two senses — their members would grow up and leave, and gangs themselves would disappear as the march of industrial modernization integrated all racial groups and eliminated the last pockets of poverty. The opposite has proved to be the case. Rather it is industrialism that has proved to be transitory, with factories and working-class jobs disappearing and gangs, and the ghettos that sustain them, becoming a permanent part of the social landscape.

While many gangs still fit Frederic Thrasher's rather innocent definition of "adolescent peer groups," the larger, more institutionalized gangs have been transformed into something quite different. They have morphed into street organizations that are important players in the life of poor communities — providing economic opportunity, dispensing "justice" and protection on a local level, controlling public space and at times becoming political players in the life of major cities. The membership has shifted somewhat with older members staying associated with the gang.

Can gangs continue to change into something other than the brutal semi-criminal hierarchies that they are at present? There are certainly tendencies in this direction. The history of the New York Almighty Latin King and Queen Nation (ALKQN) illustrates an attempt to shift a gang away from crime and violence in a self-affirming political direction, even seeking to empower female members.[12] Some African American gangs have a spiritual side influenced by the Black Muslim religion — an offshoot of traditional Islam. Other gangs have tried to enter the mainstream by building alliances with local politicians to represent community interests.

It would be easy to romanticize such tendencies. But the largely disenfranchised world of racial minorities — whether native in Winnipeg or Latino in East Los Angeles or Maori in Auckland — will continue to throw up some kind of organization to represent its interests. In an earlier era these were workers' unions, tenant organizations and political parties. Many of these organizations have been eclipsed (due to lack of results or changing conditions) or actively repressed by the authorities. In the Global South the huge squatter population has engaged in significant self-organization to demand redress in an increasingly precarious situation. In both the North and South street gangs have become important representatives of their communities. Their self-interested, violent, hyper-male approach has distorted many communities' capacity for self-assertion. But such organizations are often important social actors and they must be dealt with in ways other than just crude repression.

Gangs in Port-of-Spain, Trinidad, were revealed in 2009 to be recipients of government largesse in the form of make-work projects. Gang leaders bid on contracts to fix potholes, restore buildings and improve dilapidated services. Public shock grew as it came out that the gangs receiving support actually helped turn out the vote for the ruling People's National Party.[13]

Gangs are also involved in Brazilian favelas, where they facilitate everything from postal service to garbage disposal. There are two possible reactions to such situations: (1) cut off all official economic connections as part of a crackdown, and (2) publicize and formalize gang involvement in order to draw gangs into legitimate economic activity. Street gangs need to be engaged on a number of different levels — the criminal justice system certainly, but also at the economic and cultural levels.

In a predatory age, where self-interest is the motor force of economy and society, the youth gang's rise to prominence is hardly surprising. But what if the context were to shift? What if there were greater equality in life chances? What if significant resources (now wasted in military budgets and conspicuous consumption) were dedicated to poor urban communities? What if the illegal drug economy were taken off the table? What if obtaining small (and not so small) arms was much more difficult?

In such circumstances gangs might not disappear, but they would be affected. They would certainly shrink. Their appeal would be diminished. They might morph into semi-legitimate political projects as did the Irish and Italian gangs in the early twentieth-century urban US. Or perhaps new forms of more effective and sane community representation would squeeze them out or at least marginalize them.

Without some of these changes it seems certain that the gang threat will remain and probably increase. For as scientist Albert Einstein defined it, "insanity is doing the same thing over and over again while expecting different results." By this standard the attempt of official society to stamp out violent gangs borders on the psychotic.

Gang Vocabulary

Ausländer Gangs in Germany of Russian-German origin.

Baby gangster A young wannabe gangster between ten and twelve years of age.

Bacon or **Popo** US gang slang for the police.

Bling Jewelry, usually gold and ostentatious.

Bomb To cross out or write over another gang's graffiti or tagging.

Don The head of a gang in Jamaica.

Full bird or half bird A pound or a half-pound of cocaine.

Gruppirovka A Russian gang.

Lag sog Cantonese gang slang for extort.

Locomotive A term used by school-based groups of bullies for the head bully in the gangs of former Soviet states in Central Asia.

Meuf cool French for tough woman.

187 The number for murder in the US penal code.

Posse The name for gangs that started in Jamaica and has spread elsewhere in the Caribbean and beyond. A Haitian street gang in Montreal, for instance, is called the Crackdown Posse.

Rat pack A situation where someone is attacked by more than one person.

Sieh tao (Snakehead) Cantonese for a people-smuggling gang.

Smallie A low-level gang member.

Swarming A mass robbery carried out by a large number of usually young juveniles against a single individual in a public space.

Tagging Putting up your own gang symbol. The pitchfork is the sign for the Spanish Disciples, a Southside Chicago gang.

Tete brulée French for guy prone to fighting.

211 The number for armed robbery in the US penal code.

Zoo zoo An Uzi (Israeli machine gun).

Gangs Timeline

Tom said, "Now we'll start this band of robbers and call it Tom Sawyer's Gang. Anybody that wants to join has to take an oath, and write his name in blood."

> – Mark Twain, *The Adventures of Huckleberry Finn*, 1885.

500 BC to AD 50 In Republican Rome violent gangs of the unemployed are hired by rival senators to attack their enemies.

300s to the 1400s The Abbeys of Misrule in Western Europe battle each other for the honor of their particular abbey and to help extend its control over neighboring areas.

1200s Groups of traveling brigands rob and sometimes murder travelers in India. They are called "thuggees" from which the modern word "thug" is derived.

1800s to 1930s In the nineteenth century, in Glasgow, Scotland, Irish fighting gangs like the Caravats and the Shanavests compete with the local Penny Mobs, both engaging in extortion and robbery.

In early twentieth-century London gangs concentrated in the East End include the Yiddishers (a Jewish gang who later fought against British Nazism), the Hoxton Mob, the Watney Streeters and the Aldgate Mob.

New York and Chicago gangs are rooted in the Italian, Irish, Jewish, Polish and black communities. Immigration and the formation of "immigrant ghettos" fuel gang growth as gangs become a political force for their communities.

1950s and early 1960s The Mods and the Rockers (UK) pioneer their own styles, which are picked up by mainstream culture to market both dress and music. The cosh (a blunt metal stick) and the switchblade (or flick knife) are the weapons of choice.

The films *Rebel Without a Cause* and *The Wild One* and musicals like *West Side Story* portray gangs in the US in an era before hard drugs and semi-automatic weapons are widespread. Ethnic gang affiliation increases, as does the use of violence to defend gang turf.

Late 1960s Gangs such as the Black Panther Party, the Young Lords, La Raza and the White Panthers are half political groupings, half ethnically organized street gangs. Their activities run the spectrum from political organizing to criminal activities such as drug dealing and extortion. They create a sense of "resistance identity" that marks later street gangs after these are crushed by the police.

1980s The crack cocaine epidemic and the rise of neoliberal inequality worldwide (fueled by the Reagan and Thatcher-style attack on support for the poor) create the conditions for extensive growth of youth gang activity.

Central American gangs MS-13 and Calle 18 organize among refugee youth in LA. The gangs in Brazil's favelas start to organize.

Immigration of guest workers into Europe begins to set the conditions for gang growth.

1990s Gang activity increases in North American cities. In LA alone the number of black gangs rises from 60 in 1978 to 274 in 1996.

2000s Gangs go global, expanding under the influence of worldwide economic and labor flows. Transnational connections broaden in the areas of drugs, weapons and people-smuggling. Gang-associated violence increases with the greater availability of automatic weapons. The rapid urbanization of Southern cities creates fertile conditions for further gang growth.

Notes

1 Gangs Are Everywhere

1. Alice Winton, "Youth, Gangs and Violence," *Children's Geographies*, August 2005.
2. "Amigos dos Amigos," http://en.wikipedia.org/wiki/Amigos_dos_Amigos.
3. See www.gangnames.net for a full variety of gang names.
4. Frederic Thrasher, *The Gang: A Study of 1313 Gangs in Chicago* (Chicago: University of Chicago Press, 1927), 46.
5. Michael C. Chettleburgh, *Young Thugs: Inside the Dangerous World of Canadian Street Gangs* (Toronto: Harper Collins, 2007).
6. Mauricio Gaborit's figures are quoted from Julio Medina Murillo, "Analysis: Honduras' Violent Youth Gangs," United Press International, February 23, 2005, www12.georgetown.edu.
7. Loïc Wacquant, *Urban Outcasts: A Comparative Sociology of Advanced Marginality* (Cambridge: Polity Press, 2008).
8. John M. Hagedorn, *A World of Gangs: Armed Young Men and Gangsta Culture* (Minneapolis: University of Minnesota Press, 2008).
9. Eric Hobsbawm, *Primitive Rebels: Studies in Archaic Forms of Social Movement in the 19th and 20th Centuries* (London: Norton, 1959).
10. Ill Bill, *Ill Bill is the Future*, www.lyricsdownload.com.
11. Interview with author, Toronto, December 7, 2009.

2 Gangs and Poverty

1. http://aalbc.com/authors/black.htm. Langston Hughes, *Black Misery* (New York: Paul S. Erickson Inc, 1967).
2. *Journal of Gang Research*, National Gang Research Center, PO Box 990, Peotone, Illinois 60468-0990.
3. James Q. Wilson and Richard J. Herrnstein, *Crime and*

Human Nature (New York: The Free Press, 1985); Stanton E. Samenow, *Inside the Criminal Mind* (New York: Crown, 1984). For a critique of the "criminal mind" theory see Paul Omojo Omaji, *Responding to Youth Crime* (Sydney: Hawkins Press, 2003).

4. George L. Kelling and Catherine M. Coles, *Fixing Broken Windows: Restoring Order and Reducing Crime in Our Communities* (New York: Touchstone, 1996). For a critique see Chettleburgh, *Young Thugs*.

5. Marcus Felson, *Crime and Nature* (Thousand Oaks: Sage Publications, 2006).

6. James C. Howell, "Menacing or Mimicking? The Realities of Youth Gangs," *Juvenile and Family Court Journal*, Spring 2007.

7. Thrasher, *The Gang*, 46.

8. Richard A. Cloward and Lloyd E. Ohlin, *Delinquency and Opportunity: A Theory of Delinquent Gangs* (Glencoe: Free Press of Glencoe, 1964); Walter Miller, "Implications of Urban Lower-Class Culture for Social Work," *The Social Service Review*, Vol. 33 (1959), 219-36.

9. All figures in this box are from the UNDP *Human Development Report* 2007/2008, http://hdr.undp.org/en/reports/global/hdr2007-2008/.

10. Richard Swift, "Squatter Town," *New Internationalist*, January 2006.

11. "Chased by gang violence, residents flee Kenyan slum," *New York Times*, November 10, 2006.

12. "Guatemalan Gang Culture Conquers the Abused with Abuse," *New York Times*, April 9, 2008.

13. Chettleburgh, *Young Thugs*, 52.

3 The Underground Economy

1. Steven Levitt and Sudhir Venkatesh, "An Economic Analysis of a Drug-Selling Gang's Finances," *Quarterly Journal of Economics*, August 2000, 786.

2. "New ILO Study Says Youth Unemployment Rising," International Labour Organization, October 27, 2006, www.ilo.org.
3. "Children: Slums' First Casualties," *State of the World's Cities 2007/2008*, www.unhabitat.org.
4. "One in 31 – The Long Reach of American Corrections," Pew Center Report, March 2009, www.pewcenteronthestates.org.
5. "A Comparison of the Cost-effectiveness of the Prohibition and Regulation of Drugs," Group Transform, April 2009, www.tdpf.org.
6. Levitt and Venkatesh, "An Economic Analysis," 769.
7. Editorial, "The World's Most Dangerous Gangs," *Foreign Policy* (May 2008).
8. "The MS-13 and 18th Street Gangs: Emerging Transnational Gang Threats?" US Congressional Research Service, 2008.
9. Andre Standing, "The Social Contradictions of Organized Crime in the Cape Flats," Institute for Security Studies, Occasional Paper #74 (June 2003), 6.
10. Standing, "Social Contradictions," 6.

4 Gangs and Their Communities

1. Deborah L. Puntenney, "The Impact of Gang Violence on the Decisions of Everyday Life," *Journal of Urban Affairs*, Vol. 19, No. 2 (June 2008).
2. *Juvenile Offenders and Victims: 2006 Report* (Pittsburgh: National Center for Juvenile Justice), 82.
3. Puntenney, "Impact of Gang Violence."
4. "Police Corruption and Collusion with Gangs in Cape Town," UNHCR, Refworld, July 1999.
5. Karen Marion Dos Reis, "The Influence of Gangsterism on the Morale of Educators in the Cape Flats, Western Cape," (Dissertation.com, 2007).
6. Standing, "Social Contradictions."
7. Standing, "Social Contradictions," 5.
8. Standing, "Social Contradictions," 9.

9. Jon Lee Anderson, "Gangland," *The New Yorker*, May 10, 2009.
10. www.nationalgangcenter.gov (for US) and www.publicsafety. gc.ca (for Canada).

5 Gang Appeal

1. Paul B. Stretesky and Mark Pogrebin, "Gang Related Gun Violence: Socialization, Identity and Self," *Journal of Contemporary Ethnography* (February 2007), 103.
2. Stretesky and Pogrebin, "Gang Related Gun Violence," 104.
3. Deanna L. Wilkinson, *Guns, Violence and Identity Among African American and Latino Youth* (El Paso: LFB Scholarly Publishing, 2003).
4. Jose Luis Rocha, "Youth Gang Members and Tattoos: Stigma, Identity and Art," *Revista Envio*, No. 266 (September 2003), 6, http://www.envio.org.ni/articulo/2118.
5. Quoted in Rodrigo Bascuñán and Christian Pearce, *Enter the Babylon System: Unpacking Gun Culture from Samuel Colt to 50 Cent* (Toronto: Vintage Canada, 2007), 195.
6. Bascuñán and Pearce, *Enter the Babylon System*, 196.
7. Bascuñán and Pearce, *Enter the Babylon System*, 195.
8. See Dalton Higgins, *Hip Hop World* (Toronto: Groundwood, 2009) for a discussion of how hip hop has become the global youth subculture.
9. Oxfam-Canada, "Control Arms Media Briefing: Key Facts and Figures," March 16, 2006, www.oxfam.ca.
10. "US guns fuel Jamaican violence," *Kitchener Waterloo Record*, June 20, 2009.
11. Bascuñán and Pearce, *Enter the Babylon System*.

6 The Politics of Gangs

1. Adam Elkus, "Gangs, Terrorists and Trade," *Foreign Policy in Focus*, April 12, 2007.
2. Patrick Gavigan, "Organized Crime, Illicit Power Structures

and Guatemala's Threatened Peace Process," *International Peacekeeping* (April 2007).

3. Neilan Barnes, "Transnational Youth Gangs in Central America, Mexico and the United States," *Center for Integrated Studies* (2007).

4. Robert Muggah et al., "Urban Violence and Security Promotion in Central America," *Security Dialogue Journal* (2009).

5. Jon Lee Anderson, "Gangland."

6. "Youth, Street Gangs and Violence in South Africa," Paper given by Amanda Bissel to the international symposium on Youth, Street Culture and Urban Violence in South Africa (Abidjan, 1997).

7. Issue Brief, "Groups, Gangs and Armed Violence in Timor-Leste," *Small Arms Survey*, April 17, 2009, www.smallarmssurvey.org.

8. Peter Muello, "Corruption Scandal," *AP Worldstream*, May 29, 2008, www.apworldstream.org.

9. ICRC, "Poverty a Breeding Ground for Violence in Cité Soleil," May 1, 2009, www.icrc.org.

7 The Assault on Youth

1. Bernardine Dohrn, coeditor with William Ayers, Rick Ayers and Jesse L. Jackson, *Zero Tolerance: Resisting the Drive for Punishment in Our Schools: A Handbook for Parents, Students, Educators, and Citizens*, www.stanford.edu/group/cubberley/node/3669.

2. Yemi Babalola, "Makoko Residents and their unwanted guests," January 5, 2009, http://allafrica.com/stories/200905010060.html.

3. Wacquant, *Urban Outcasts*.

4. Interview with author, Toronto, July 12, 2009.

5. Diane Lefer, "Juvenile In/Justice and Proposition 6," *LA Progressive*, October 17, 2008.

6. "Zero Tolerance Policy Report," American Bar Association

(February 2001), www.abanet.org/crimjust/juvjus/
   zerotolreport.html.

7. Evan Williams, "Death to Undesirables," *The Independent*,
   May 15, 2009.

8. Human Rights Watch, "Lethal Force, Police Violence and
   Public Security in Rio de Janerio and São Paulo," 2009,
   www.hrw.org.

9. www.citymayors.com/society/usa-youth-curfews.html.

10. www.statewatch.org. See ASBOwatch.

11. Chettleburgh, *Young Thugs*.

12. "Violence Against Children in Conflict with the Law," The
    Howard League for Penal Reform, 2008, www.dei-france.
    org.

13. Molly McDonough, "Report: Recidivism Higher for Youth
    Offenders Tried as Adults," *ABA Journal*, November 30, 2007.

14. www.transparency.org. See Corruption Perceptions Index.

15. www.escapefromthesmugosphere.wordpress.com. Search
    Camatte.

16. www.monthlyreview.org/598einstein.

8. A Future with Gangs

1. www.genevadeclaration.org.

2. Patrick Fitzsimmons, "The politics of corruption in the 21st
   Century," www.globalization.icaap.org.

3. Chettleburgh, *Young Thugs*.

4. Chettleburgh, *Young Thugs*.

5. John Seabrook, "Don't Shoot: A Radical Approach to Gang
   Violence," *The New Yorker*, June 22, 2009.

6. Robert Muggah, "Urban Violence and Violence Reduction
   in Central America," *Security Dialogue Journal*, 2009.

7. www.vivario.org.br.

8. "Viva Rio in Haiti: Research and Papers,"
   www.comunidadesegura.org/en.

9. Judith Greene and Kevin Pranis, "Gang Wars: The Failure

of Enforcement Tactics and the Need for Effective Public Safety Strategics," *Justice Policy Institute Report*, July 2007 (Washington, DC), www.justicepolicy.org.

10. www.homeboy-industries.org.

11. www.gunpolicy.org.

12. Luis Barrios, "Gangs and Spirituality of Liberation," in John Hagedorn, ed., *Gangs in the Global City: Alternatives to Traditional Criminology* (Urbana and Chicago: University of Illinois Press, 2007).

13. Dorn Townsend and Robert Muggah, "Tackling Violence on Trinidad's Mean Streets," www.smallarmssurvey.org.

For Further Information

Books

Bascuñán, Rodrigo and Christian Pearce. *Enter the Babylon System: Unpacking Gun Culture from Samuel Colt to 50 Cent.* Toronto: Vintage Canada, 2007.

Chettleburgh, Michael C. *Young Thugs: Inside the Dangerous World of Canadian Street Gangs.* Toronto: Harper Collins, 2007.

Fleisher, Mark S. *Beggars and Thieves: Lives of Urban Street Criminals.* Madison: University of Wisconsin Press, 1995.

Hagedorn, John M. *A World of Gangs: Armed Young Men and Gangsta Culture.* Minneapolis: University of Minnesota Press, 2008.

Hagedorn, John M., ed. *Gangs in the Global City: Alternatives to Traditional Criminology.* Urbana and Chicago: University of Illinois Press, 2007.

Journal of Gang Research. National Gang Crime Research Center, PO Box 990, Peotone, IL 60468-0990.

Moreno, Tony. *Lessons from a Gang Cop.* Toronto: Astwood, 2005.

Omaji, Paul Omojö. *Responding to Youth Crime: Towards Radical Criminal Justice Partnerships.* Sydney: Hawkins Press, 2003.

Venkatesh, Sudhir. *Gang Leader for a Day: A Rogue Sociologist Takes to the Streets.* New York: Penguin, 2008.

Films and TV Series

Boyz in the Hood, directed by John Singleton (1991). A Los Angeles street gang movie with numerous rappers.

City of God (Cidade de Deus), directed by Fernando Meirelles and Kátia Lund (2003). A Brazilian crime drama set in the slums of Rio de Janeiro.

Colors, directed by Dennis Hopper (1988; Orion Pictures Corporation). Starring Sean Penn and Robert Duvall, and set in Los Angeles.

Ross Kemp on Gangs, produced by Ross Kemp (2006-2009). A series of seventeen television documentaries set all over the world.

Sin Nombre (Without Name), directed by Cary Fukunaga (2009).
A film about Mexican and Central American Maras.
The Wire, created by David Simon (2002-2008). HBO television
series set in Baltimore.

Websites

www.gangresearch.net A thoughtful approach to gangs worldwide.
www.gangstyle.com Testimonials by gang members and ex-members.
www.smallarmssurvey.org An organization campaigning against the
small arms trade.
www.knowgangs.com An online history of gangs.
www.csdpp.org; www.drugpolicy.org Websites advocating a com-
monsense approach to drug policy.

Acknowledgments

Thanks to Ken Epps of Project Ploughshares, and Robert Muggah and Jennifer H. Hazen of the Small Arms Survey in Geneva.

Index

Abbeys of Misrule, 13
Afghanistan, 47, 113
Africa, 33. *See also specific countries*
West Africa, 47, 54, 89, 90
African Americans, 50
African National Congress, 60, 85
alienation, 34–35, 115
Almighty Latin King and Queen Nation, 123
America's Army (video game), 72
Amigos dos Amigos, 9, 52
Anderson, Craig, 72
Anti-Social Behaviour Act (UK, 2003), 101–2
apartheid, 14, 60, 85
APREDE, 117
Area Boys, 96
Ariès, Philippe, 93
Aristide, Jean-Bertrand, 90 91
Aryan Brotherhood, 67
ASBOs, 101–2
Avery, John, 46

bailes, 76
Bangladesh, 44
Bascuñán, Rodrigo, 74–75
Belgium, 11
"big gang" theory, 29–30
Big L, 74
Black Panther Party, 84
Blackstone Rangers, 84
Blair, Tony, 101
Bloods. *See* Los Angeles

Bloods and Crips Shooting (video), 24
blowback, 17–18, 91
Blowes, Stephen, 101
Body Count (Ice-T), 78
Borgelin, Prospere, 91
Boston, MA, 116–17
Boyle, Greg, 120
Brazil, 33, 73, 85, 100, 118
community involvement in, 37, 52–53, 124
corruption in, 87, 105
gangs in, 9, 76, 103
Rio de Janeiro, 9, 52–53, 88, 118
São Paulo, 52
Britain. *See* United Kingdom
British National Party, 35
"broken windows" theory, 28, 98
Bulletproof (video game), 72
Burma (Myanmar), 44

Cairney, Patrick and Louis, 101–2
California, 17–18, 28, 39, 66, 97–98. *See also* Los Angeles
Calle 18, 16, 83
Camatte, Jacques, 105
Canada, 31, 65, 97, 122
capitalism, 54, 106–7, 109–10. *See also* economy
Caribbean, 75, 124. *See also specific countries*

Central America, 87. *See also specific countries*
anti-gang tactics, 115, 117–18
and drug trade, 47, 48, 82
gangs in, 12–13, 17, 38–39
guns in, 81, 86
immigrants from, 83
protest in, 81–83
Chettleburgh, Michael, 40, 103–4
Chicago, IL, 15, 31, 58, 84
Chicago School, 32–33
children, 93–94. *See also* youth
as soldiers, 88–90
as workers, 44, 93
Chris D, 75
Cincinnati, OH, 10
cities
no-go areas, 96
slums in, 35–37, 96
squatter communities, 16, 36–37, 43, 58–62, 123
youth in, 15–16, 41–42
clothing, 69–71
cocaine, 47, 48, 82. *See also* crack cocaine
Coles, Catherine, 28
Colombia, 47, 100, 113
colors, 70–71
Comando Vermelho (Red Command), 52–53, 76, 85
communities, 118

anti-gang activities, 61, 71, 98–100
gang involvement in, 37, 52–53, 54, 124
gangs and, 56–67, 108–9
gangs as voice of, 37, 52–53, 62, 123–24
squatters as, 16, 36–37, 43, 58–62, 123
Contras, 81
corruption, 95, 105
fight against, 111, 112
in governments, 87–92
of police, 87–88, 92, 112, 115
Costa Rica, 13
crack cocaine, 48, 49–50, 82
crime, 44–49. *See also* drug trade; guns
as gang income source, 48, 54, 60–61
risks, 50, 54–55
youth and, 95, 101–2
Crime and Nature (Felson), 29–30
Crips. *See* Los Angeles
curfews, 100–101

Darrow, Clarence, 108
Denmark, 67
de Soto, Hernando, 45
Dissel, Amanda, 85–86
dissing, 69
Dohrn, Bernardine, 93
drugs, 46, 90, 97. *See also* drug trade; *specific drugs*
decriminalization of,

111–12, 113–14
war on, 46–47, 111–15
drug trade
in Central America, 47, 48, 82
effects, 114–15
gangs and, 48–51, 62
in Mexico, 47, 111–12
in South Africa, 60–62
and violence, 50–51

East Timor, 9, 86–87
Eastwood, Clint, 30
Eazy-E, 74
economy. *See also* capitalism; poverty
as cause of gangs, 80–81
of gangs, 49–51, 54–55, 62
globalization of, 65
and poverty, 110–11
underground, 44–48
education, 94, 99
Einstein, Albert, 106–7, 125
Elkus, Adam, 80
El Salvador, 33, 71, 81, 118. *See also* Maras
gangs in, 12, 13, 17, 83
England. *See* United Kingdom
Enter the Babylon System (Bascuñán and Pearce), 74–75
Escobar, Pablo, 47
Ethiopia, 44
Europe, 43, 46, 104. *See also specific*

countries
gangs in, 11, 13, 109
Evens (gang leader), 91
extortion, 52, 54, 60

failed states, 88. *See also specific countries*
La Familia, 67
FARC, 113
FBI, 84
Felson, Marcus, 29–30
Fernandinho (gang leader), 64
50 Cent, 72, 74
France, 35, 43, 104, 122
gangs in, 11, 41–42, 58
"Fuck tha Police" (N.W.A.), 74

Gaborit, Mauricio, 12–13
The Gang (Thrasher), 11–12, 31
Gang Deterrence and Community Protection Act (US, 2005), 97
gangs. *See also* youth
as aberration, 32–33
adult, 11, 48–49, 62
and adult world, 62–64, 104–7
alternatives to, 118–20
conflict between, 23–24, 49–50, 60–61, 116–17, 119
context of, 11, 31
cultural influence, 22–23, 69, 73–76, 78–79
definition, 18–20

ethnicity and, 31, 65
as family substitute,
69, 71–72
female members,
38–39, 123
foot soldiers, 49, 50,
54–55
future of, 122–25
as glamorous,
20–23, 50, 72, 75
growth of, 26–27
habitat, 57–59
history, 13, 20–21,
80, 92, 127–28
as identity source,
23, 69, 105–6
institutionalized, 19,
20, 52–54, 59–62,
63–64, 122–23
leaders, 49, 62, 64, 73
membership in,
12–13, 53, 57, 60
names for, 9–10, 18,
60
organization of,
11–12
as political force,
52–53, 87, 105–6,
123
preventive measures,
24–25, 116–18
in prisons, 102–4
reasons for joining,
8, 26–27, 64, 68–79
responses to, 27–30,
61, 71, 80–92, 94,
98–100
signifiers, 69–73
stereotyping of,
29–30
studies of, 31–33, 34
support for, 21–22,
61–62

theories about,
27–30, 98
vocabulary, 126
websites about, 10,
24
gangsta rap, 22–23,
73–76, 78
Geddes, James, 46
Geneva Declaration on
Armed Violence
and Development
(2006), 108
genocide, 82
Germany, 10, 11, 34, 35
skinhead gangs in,
65–66, 87
Gini, Corrado, 32
Gini index, 32–33
girls, 44
in gangs, 38–39, 123
Giuliani, Rudy, 98
globalization
of economy, 65
of gangs, 69–73
Global North, 19–20,
33, 53. See also spe-
cific countries
Global South, 43–44,
45, 48. See also spe-
cific countries
gangs in, 8, 31–32,
70–71
poverty in, 31–32,
43–44
squatter communi-
ties in, 16, 36–37,
43, 58–59, 123
governments. See also
specific countries
corrupt, 87–92
gangs as part of, 87
protests against,
81–85

responses to gangs,
29–30
graffiti, 71–73
Gran Torino (film), 30
Guatemala, 33
corruption in, 87–88
gangs in, 13, 38–39,
83
protest in, 81–82
responses to gangs,
71, 100, 117
guns, 76–79, 90
availability, 121, 122
campaigns against,
118, 120–22
in Central America,
81, 86
manufacturers, 77,
78, 121
in rap music, 74–75
from United States,
77–78, 81
Guzman, Joaquin "El
Chapo," 47

Hagedorn, John M.,
18–19
Haiti, 33, 90–91, 105,
118–19
Hampton, Fred, 84
Heston, Charlton, 78
hip hop culture, 22–23,
73–76
Hobsbawm, Eric,
20–21
Homeboy Industries, 120
Homies Unidos, 118
Honduras, 33, 81,
117–18
gangs in, 12–13, 17,
83
Honor and Respect for
Bel Air, 119

housing projects, 41–42, 57–58

Ice-T, 78
identity, 23, 69, 105–6
immigrants, 17–18, 31, 34–35, 65
incarceration, 46, 95, 101, 102–4
India, 13
indigenous peoples, 14, 31
inequality, 32–33, 110–11. *See also* poverty
International Narcotics Board, 46
International Opium Commission, 46
Ireland, 43
Israel, 67
Italy, 43, 104

Jamaica, 9, 77–78, 91–92
JHAJA, 117–18
Johnson, Robert L., 104
Journal of Gang Research, 26

Kelling, George, 28
Kennedy, David, 117
Kenya, 33, 36–37, 54
King, Martin Luther, 83–84
King, Rodney, 22
KRS-One, 75

Lambeth, Jack, 101
Latin America, 9, 11, 58–59, 101–2. *See also specific regions and countries*
United States and,

81–82, 113
law-and-order lobby, 27–29, 94
Liberia, 89, 90
Lins, Álvaro, 88
Lord's Resistance Army, 89
Los Angeles, CA, 74, 116, 120
  as exporter of gang culture, 16–17, 83
  gangs in, 15, 21–22, 66, 70
Lowriders, 66

mano dura policies, 115, 117–18
Maras, 16–18, 38–39, 53, 71
  in United States, 16, 66, 83
Mara Salvatrucha, 16, 83
masculinity, 23, 68–69
media, 29–30
Metzger, Tom, 67
Mexico, 75, 78
  corruption in, 87, 105, 112
  and drug trade, 47, 111–12
microcredit, 45
Mods, 14–15
Montreal Preventive Treatment Program, 25
Montt, Ríos, 82
Moreno, Tony, 116
Mungiki Gang, 36–37, 54
music, 22–23, 73–76, 78

Namibia, 32

narcocorridos, 75
National Democratic Party (Germany), 35
National Rifle Association (US), 78
neoliberalism, 42, 94, 110–11
neo-Nazis, 10, 35, 66
Nepal, 44
Newton, Huey, 84
New York City, 119, 121, 123
  crime rate, 28, 98
New Zealand, 14, 31
Nicaragua, 83
  gangs in, 13, 37, 70–71
  protest in, 81, 82
Nigeria, 12, 33, 96
Notorious B.I.G. (aka Biggie Smalls), 74
N.W.A. (Niggaz With Attitude), 74

Obama, Barack, 78
opium, 46, 47
outlaws, 20–21

pandillas, 37, 70, 83
Papua New Guinea, 33
Pearce, Christian, 74–75
People Against Gangsterism and Drugs (PAGAD), 61
Petitioners, 86–87
Poland, 67
police, 84, 120. *See also* crime; incarceration
  anti-gang tactics, 96–97, 115–18
  corrupt, 87–88, 92, 112, 115

gangs as part of, 87, 91–92

political systems, 35, 80–92
    gangs as part of, 52–53, 105–6, 123
    response to gangs, 11, 85–87

poverty, 94, 110–11. *See also* inequality
    gangs as response to, 26–55, 63

predators, 54, 106–7, 109–11

Primeiro Comando da Capital, 52, 103

prisons, 102–4. *See also* incarceration

Proibidão music, 76

projects (housing), 41–42, 57–58

prostitution, 44

protection rackets, 45, 52

protest, 81–85, 94–95

Public Enemy (rap group), 75

Public Enemy No. 1 (gang), 66

racism, 30, 82, 95
    as gang focus, 27, 35, 65–67
    gangs as response to, 14, 21–22

Ramos-Horta, José, 86

rap music, 22–23, 73–76, 78

Reagan, Ronald, 80, 81–82

reggae music, 75

religion, 11, 123

Rockers, 14–15

Russia, 10, 66, 67, 109

Ruthless Records, 74

Samenow, Stanton, 27–29

Sandinistas, 81, 82, 83

San Francisco, CA, 28

scavengers, 107

Schwarzkopf, Norman, 23

"Self-Destruction" (Public Enemy), 75

sexuality, 94

Shakur, Tupac, 74

Sierra Leone, 89, 90

skinheads, 10, 35, 65–66

Slovakia, 32

slums, 35–37, 96. *See also* housing projects; squatter communities

social cleansing, 98–100

social justice, 81–85, 111

social welfare, 11, 42, 58, 94

South Africa, 33, 105
    Cape Flats, 10, 54, 60–62
    drug trade in, 60–62
    gangs in, 10, 14, 54, 60–62, 85–86

Southeast Asia, 9, 44, 54, 86–87

Spain, 11, 35, 43

Spider Girls, 39

squatter communities, 16, 36–37, 43, 58–62, 123

Standing, Andre, 54, 61–62

Straight Outta Compton (N.W.A.), 74

Street Gangs Book Club, 26

Sweden, 104

tagging, 71–73

Taiwan, 54

Taliban, 113

tattoos, 70–71

"taxing," 45, 52

Taylor, Charles, 89

Terceiro Comando Puro (Pure Third Command), 52, 64

Thailand, 44, 54

Thatcher, Margaret, 80

Thrasher, Frederic, 11–12, 31

thuggees, 13

Toronto, ON, 97

Transform, 46

Trinidad, 124

tsotsi, 14

25 to Life (video game), 72

Uganda, 44, 89

underemployment, 41, 42–43

unemployment, 42–44, 50, 60

United Kingdom, 35
    gangs in, 11, 14–15, 65, 67
    youth control measures, 101–2, 104

United Nations, 46, 47

United States, 33. *See also* California; *specific cities*
    corruption in, 92, 105
    curfews in, 100–101

damaging policies, 17–18, 58, 83
gangs in, 12, 14, 39, 92
gun culture, 78, 99, 121–22
as gun source, 77–78, 81
immigrants in, 17–18, 34, 83
incarceration rates, 103, 112
inequality in, 58, 83–84
and Latin America, 81–82, 113
Maras in, 16, 66, 83
poverty in, 58, 96
race and gangs in, 50, 65, 66–67
and war on drugs, 46, 112, 113
Urban Outcasts (Wacquant), 15

Veblen, Thorstein, 106
Venezuela, 120
video games, 72
vigilantes, 61, 71, 98–100
violence
    as cultural compo-
nent, 72, 76, 105
    drug trade and, 50–51
    inter-gang, 23–24, 49–50, 60–61, 116–17, 119
    in rap music, 74, 78
    romanticization of, 74–75
Viva Rio, 118

Wacquant, Loïc, 15
Walt, Scott, 46
warlords, 88
war on drugs, 46–47, 111–15
warriors, 23, 49
Washington, DC, 121–22
welfare (social), 11, 42, 58, 94
white supremacists, 27, 65–67
Why Socialism? (Einstein), 106–7
Wilkinson, Deanna, 69
Wilson, James Q., 27–29
The Wire (TV series), 24
women, 44
    in gangs, 38–39, 123
A World of Gangs

(Hagedorn), 18–19

xenophobia, 65–66. *See also* immigrants; racism

youth. *See also* children; gangs; zero-tolerance policies
    in cities, 15–16, 41–42
    as criminals, 95, 101–2
    get-tough approach, 28–29, 97–98, 115, 117–18
    incarceration of, 95, 101, 102–4
    as outcasts, 15–16
    programs for, 118, 119
    as revolutionaries, 94–95
    sanctions against, 100–102

zero-tolerance policies, 25, 95, 98–99
    and blowback, 17–18, 91
    as failure, 25, 117
Zhu Lien Bang, 54